THE INFLUENCER EFFECT

INSIDER TIPS FOR GEARING UP YOUR ONLINE SUCCESS

BY

GREG JAMESON

With Forewords by

James Malinchak

Armand Morin

Steve Olsher

Andrea Vahl

Joel Comm

Ken McArthur

Contribution by Judith Briles

Published by WebStores Ltd.
www.WebStoresLtd.com

ISBN: 978-0-9991727-0-4

Advanced Praise for
"The Influencer Effect"

The Influencer Effect is a smart and strong strategy for developing the SYSTEMS you need to run a successful ecommerce business. Using his proprietary GEARS system, Greg breaks down the complexities into manageable and implementable steps to message, market and sell products online. The book is chock full of real-life situations and stories. I've been selling online for over 17 years, and the GEARS system is the first of its kind to really help you understand ALL of the moving parts. Simply brilliant. Get it.

Stephanie Frank
International Best Selling Author,
The "Accidental" Millionaire.
www.Stephaniefrank.com

This book is a must read for anyone wanting to launch an ecommerce business or has a new one that is not creating the results you want. This week I shared the book with a client and she is so much in love that she offered to gift me a spa treatment! The 80 secrets to ecommerce success is easily explained and outlined.

Jessica Peterson
Simply WOW Agency
http://simplywowagency.com

Greg is an influencer marketing genius, being able to take a complex subject and reducing it to simple, actionable steps that anyone can replicate. Following on the success of his previous book, Greg totally nails it with "The Influencer Effect". As he states in the book, nothing is new in internet marketing, but it can be very time consuming and complex. He shows you how he has used everyday people to influence the results for his own websites and that of his clients. If you are looking for ways to get other people to market on your behalf, this is a must-read book.

Patrick Snow
International Best-Selling Author and Keynote Speaker
http://patricksnow.com

If you have a website, you need this book. If you do any type of online marketing, you need this book. If you want to influence your audience to buy from you, refer you to their friends or share what you do on social media, you need this book. Greg pulls out all the stops with "The Influencer Effect" and shows you exactly what you need to do to attract customers into your funnel. It's a fantastic book filled with real world examples that you can emulate to create your influence.

Rob Anspach
Founder Anspach Media
www.AnspachMedia.com

As an internet marketing expert, Greg provides a blueprint with steps to follow for making your website an attraction magnet to customers. The Influencer Effect should be on everyone's shelf as a guide to increasing your specific influence for your customers. This system approach to provide you with real world examples will help you understand how to do business online. Be hungry and devour this knowledge and become an influencer, too!

Dr. Gene Munson
Founder Eagles Nest Communications
www.ENCPresents.com

Greg Jameson is one of the world's foremost experts on getting others to market and sell on your behalf. This is known as the influencer effect, and this book by that title reveals how you too can leverage this important marketing technique. I've read lots of books, and this is one of the best marketing books I've ever read. If you've ever wondered how to really put an effective marketing campaign in place using digital media, you will not only want to read this book, but refer to it time after time.

Dr. Marlene Bizub
Psychotherapist and Professional Speaker
www.marlenebizub.com

Greg Jameson in The Influencer Effect answers the question why, when people just look for the magic tools to bring success to their ecommerce site, they fail! Greg shares how it's not just information and tools that leads to success but the magic is having a proven system to implement the tools. Greg will take you by the hand and walk you step-by-step through his revolutionary system. This will be your personal roadmap that will allow your perfect client to see you as their perfect solution. If you're truly ready to be an influencer in your market and make a huge impact, then The Influencer Effect will be your secret sauce to success.

Gary Barnes
International #1 best-selling author,
International Speaker & Business Coach
www.GaryBarnesInternational.com

The Influencer Effect by Greg Jameson is a refreshing and compelling perspective on influencing your audience and reaching the desired goal by leveraging your connections to make a lasting impact! Greg's GEARS Method is simple yet brilliant and must do, not only to survive, but also to thrive in today's ever so changing the digital world.

Izabela Lundberg
Executive Coach,
International Best-Selling Author & Keynote Speaker
http://IzabelaLundberg.com

I'm one of the lucky ones – Greg Jameson is a friend as well as a superb mentor, helping me with my successful online presence. I've known Greg for several years and I have always been impressed with his keen insights when it comes to the internet. That's one of the reasons our mastermind group named him 'the master of the digital universe.' Many people claim to be expert, but Greg knows what he's talking about.

In this book, Greg shares his real-time, everyday web marketing experience with a view toward profit and effectiveness. His influence model serves businesses of all sizes.

Greg has the success stories to prove it, too. In fact, I'd say that he 'wrote the book' on it long before he put his knowledge and experience into print. This fun and informative book packs decades of knowledge into a concise and valuable read.

Mitch Krayton
Travel Concierge
Make Memories, Not Regrets™
www.KraytonTravel.com

Whether you are a strategist, tactical implementer, "average joe" or a marketing professional, this book will leave you in awe by how much you didn't know about the power of a deliberately developed e-commerce strategy. It is rare that any modern-day e-commerce or internet marketing guru started at the beginning of personal computers and then continued with a focused obsession for decades. With over 30 years of experience packed into one place, we are truly privileged that Greg has written The Influencer Effect for the rest of us. This comprehensive guide filled with techniques, tips and strategies, will inspire you beyond the limits of what you thought possible for your business.

Dani Espinosa
Entrepreneur
www.linkedin.com/in/daniespinosa/

The world is changing, and being adaptable is now more important than ever. Adapting new technologies is crucial if you want your business to thrive in a digital ecosystem that is constantly evolving. The Influencer Effect is a blueprint for doing just that. Greg has an impressive amount of experience and wisdom to share, which beautifully complements his practical approach to building your brand in an increasingly competitive landscape. Woven into his central thesis are empirical pieces of information that make this book not only innovative and insightful, but also refreshingly pragmatic.

Bob Kittell
Memory and Communications Expert
UltraMemory.org

My excellent friend, Greg Jameson, has done it again! In his latest book, "The Influencer Effect", he has masterfully crafted an easy to use system, which will take the trial and error out of your ability to attract attention, through to getting your products and services sold online. He explains what it takes to make a successful sale and how to deliver a system which will ensure that you get consistent, lasting results.

For those who are starting to set up an online business, buying this book will give you a huge advantage which will make those around you astonished at how quickly and effectively you have grown your business. I am certain that those who have had an online business for sometime, are also set to benefit considerably, as you discover many gems that I feel sure are set to make a huge difference. I am one of the lucky ones to have had this book fall into my hands, as it is certain to have a dramatic positive effect on my business, my influence and ultimately my sales. Why not join me and be one of the "lucky ones" too!?

Andy W. Shepherd
Peak Performance and Breakthrough Coach
http://ShepherdCoaching.com

The Influencer Effect by Greg Jameson is a book that everyone can understand how to grow their business. I am so glad that he has written this book. It is such a trending idea that needed to be shared with the world. The GEARS strategy he created is G=Generate Interest, E- Empower Influencers, A=Amplify your message, R=Results, S=Strategy. Greg Jameson is a brilliant marketer that has taken the mystery out of success. I highly recommend this book if you want to grow your business.

Tracy Malone
Digital Marketing Consultant
www.TracyAMalone.com

There are thousands and thousands of books about marketing and business success. Once in a while there is a book that is easy to understand, practical and full of real advice that works in the real world. Greg Jameson has written such a book.

The Influencer Effect is a rare find that will help beginners and experienced entrepreneurs learn how to create real value, increase visibility and generate income in the fast-changing world of the digital economy.

Unless you are determined to do everything the hard way, you should read this book, and implement the principles, NOW.

Kellan Fluckiger, The Ultimate Catalyst
#1 best-selling Author, Speaker and Coach
Creator of 'The Results Equation'
www.resultsequationintensive.com

What a gift Greg Jameson has delivered to the business community with his newest book "The Influencer Effect"! Greg has the unique ability to take seemingly complex business ideas and reduce them so anyone can understand them. Don't think for a second that he's "dumbing down" anything. What he's doing is reducing concepts to their core principles. Which is really what all visionaries do. His "GEAR System" is brilliant. And at a true Influencer's core, lies the ability and willingness to deliver massive value. Greg has certainly delivered massive value with "The Influencer Effect". Use this book as a road map to navigate the success of your business. And remember that small activities repeated consistently over time produce massive results. Thanks Greg for this gem of a book.

Kevin Knebl, CMEC
The Most Recommended Business Speaker in the World
CEO - Knebl Communications, LLC
www.KevinKnebl.com

Contents

FOREWORD by James Malinchak

The power of influence, especially when it comes to making purchasing decisions, may be one of the most sought-after means of getting people to buy into what you are selling. Yet it is also one of the most misunderstood ways of marketing your products and services. Most of us think, "Wouldn't it be great if I could get a celebrity to endorse my business?" This is like thinking, "Wouldn't it be great if I could get listed on page one of Google?" Neither of these things by themselves guarantees your success. In fact, this type of "if-only thinking", that magic will happen in your business, is the cause of most online business never realizing their potential. The truth is that most online businesses fail. People put up new websites every day and never sell anything.

That's a pretty sobering way to start out a motivational book, but once you understand that an online business is just that, a business, and that you have to work it just like any other business in order to succeed, then you will appreciate the GEARS system that Greg has provided in this transformational book. Influence is in fact huge, but not in the way that you might imagine. When I was on ABCs hit show, The Secret Millionaire, I lived in Gary, Indiana for a week as if I was on welfare. But I ended up touching the lives of individuals who had no knowledge of who I was. Since then, I've leveraged the influence that came with this notoriety.

People often ask me how I get so many people to attend my live events. My response is always the same, *"I don't know one way to get 500 people to register for my events. But I know 50 ways to get 10 people to register and I do them all!"*

That is what marketing is all about. In this book, you will discover multiple ways to market your products or services. It's like having a website. One website may not generate 100 sales a month for you. But what if you had 10 websites that each generated 10 sales a month for you? Then, what if you spread out your marketing messages so that different influencers were attracting different buyers to each website? Often, success is not a single hit, but a series of doing many small things over an extended period of time. So how do you get not just one influencer, but multiple influencers making an impact on your business?

I've discovered that influence is not something you buy, but something you earn. Many celebrities and thought-leaders speak at my events, and their influence helps attract people to attend those events. The reason is because those celebrities have become friends who "know, like, and trust me," a phrase created 30+ years ago by Bob Burg.

That is crucial in today's business environment. You must get others to know, like, and trust you. One of the best ways to do this is to meet people in real life. Attend live events, like mine, and get to know the other people. Establish relationships with them. Perhaps after a period of time, they will become friends and colleagues. As Greg points out in this book, experts and friends often have a higher level of influence than a celebrity does. One of the first things he suggests is that you provide something of significant value to others, for free, in order to over-deliver. Figure out how you can add value to the lives of the people you meet. Get to know them as individuals. Then, and only then, will you be able to use their influence to help grow your business.

That is one of the things Greg has done with his book, The Influencer Effect. He has borrowed the influence of others by featuring them at the beginning of each section. The message and the stories in this book are powerful enough to stand on their own without needing the influence of these individuals, but it is strengthened by the fact that Greg is using this technique as an example.

This book is a fun and interesting read. It is full of intriguing stories that may cause you to keep reading straight through until you finish the book in one sitting. The GEARS system that Greg describes shows you how you can implement the Influencer Effect in your business (yes, you are going to have to work the system in order to discover the magic). It is not intended as a technical how-to book, but rather a book to stimulate your mind. How can I get others to market and sell on my behalf, and how can I leverage their influence to generate massive profits for my business? You are about to learn exactly that.

James Malinchak

Featured on ABC's Hit TV Show, *"Secret Millionaire"*
"One of America's Most Requested Motivational Business Speakers"
Delivered 3,000+ Talks ● 1,000+ Consultations ● Authored 20+ Books
Founder, www.BigMoneySpeaker.com

Preface

Being an influencer wasn't even a thing ten years ago. Referrals, of course, have been with us as long as humans have been marketing their products and services to others. And referrals are great, but often sporadic and unreliable. But what if there was a way to exponentially increase referrals or awareness on a consistent basis? That method is already here: it's called influencer marketing. While some people refer to themselves as influencers, most influencers are simply people doing what they love to do and sharing their findings with their followers. They are givers. They don't set out to become an influencer, but rather, they share their experiences, and those experiences have an effect on how consumers make purchasing decisions.

Most people are aware that major brands hire movie stars, singers, and athletes to promote their products. But few of us want to be told by multi-millionaires what kind of shoes we should be wearing or what we should get our moms for Mother's Day. We all know that these celebrities get paid substantial amounts of money for their endorsements. Many of them make more money for their endorsements than they do for their "real" jobs. Such celebrities are called macro-influencers, because they reach a large number of people. Yet most do an ineffective job of convincing people like you and me to actually make a purchase.

Subject-matter experts and social influencers on the other hand do much better job of connecting with people who are likely to take action based upon their recommendations. This is known as the influencer effect. These folks are called micro-influencers. Micro-influencers, as the name suggests, are influencers who have a significant but not massive following as compared to big-name celebrities. They are individuals who are considered to be experts in their relevant niche. Bloggers, YouTubers, and Instagrammers that create content about a specific subject are examples. They are usually passionate about their respective categories and are looked to as reliable sources of information and recommendations on purchases related to those categories. As such, they are more reliable than simple consumer reviews. Using multiple micro-influencers often produces bigger outcomes than a single macro-influencer can.

So, how do you build influencer marketing into your marketing plan? The leading ecommerce professionals know that digital marketing is more than just creating a sales funnel – all your marketing efforts must work together like a well-oiled machine. Chief among these methods is getting others to recommend your products and services to their friends. You need a system that incorporates this into your overall marketing efforts. The GEARS system described in this book shows you how to do just that. When you do, the results can be massive. Whether you are a company or a leader looking to have others generate content and share it with their followers, or you are an expert who is sharing knowledge for something you are passionate about, influencer marketing is here to stay.

Acknowledgements

In addition to the traditional "foreword", each section has its own foreword. These were written by friends and colleagues from whom I borrowed their influence. I am extremely grateful to Armand Morin, Steve Olsher, Andrea Vahl, Joel Comm, and Ken McArthur for lending their names and expertise to my project. Of course, I am also grateful to my friend James Malinchak, for writing the overall book foreword, and to all those who wrote such complimentary testimonials for this book.

No book would be possible without the help of a great editor, and my friend Helen Gaus did an incredible job of making this book more readable and enjoyable for you. I am indebted to her for the time and effort she took to make my words come alive.

And finally, I must thank my wife and business partner, Jill. She not only put up with me spending countless hours writing this manuscript and reading it, but she is equally responsible for many of the examples I have used in this book.

Introduction

"What you do EVERYDAY matters more than what you do ONCE IN A WHILE."

- Gretchen Rubin
Author and Blogger

When I was in high school back in the mid 1970's, I had a very unusual situation. I took a course in BASIC programming – the school had a single teletype machine with a paper tape reader that was connected to the county's mainframe, a DEC PDP-10. What made my situation unique though, was that my father was a professor at Colorado State University where he had a research project. This project allowed him to bring home a portable teletype machine that had a built-in coupler modem, where I could dial into the county mainframe using my school's account. Since they were not expecting anyone to use this account during any time other than the schedule class at school, there were no limitations – I could access the computer without restriction (and I did, racking up hundreds of hours on the machine). Basically, this meant that I was doing home computing about a decade before anyone else!

For the class that I was taking, we were supposed to write a program for our end-of-semester project. I chose to create a "game" that simulated someone on a downhill ski run. But I had a dilemma: every time you ran the program, you got the exact same results. I wanted the results to be different, so that you would get a unique experience each time you played the game. My teacher told me about the RAN function, a random number generator and suggested that I use that. But the number returned by the random number generator was also the same each time. It just looked up a number between 0 and 1 (out to about 12 decimal places), from a table of random numbers and returned that number. Then it hit me! What if I multiplied the random number times the current time like this:

$$RAN * Val[Hour(now)] * Val[Minute(now)] * Val[Second(now)]$$

I may not have remembered the exact syntax after all these years, but the concept was to multiply the random number from the table by the current time value to get a number that was different every time. I was informed that this wasn't really a random value, because time wasn't random. But that didn't matter – what mattered was that it worked! This was my first computer "hack." I made the computer do something that it wasn't designed to do. Interestingly, this method for getting random results is still used by many programmers all these years later.

The reason for sharing this story with you is to share with you that I've been involved in the computer software industry longer than most people on this planet. Of course, there were other individuals that also had early exposure to computers during this time: Bill Gates (who also learned to program on a DEC PDP-10), Steve Jobs, Bill Joy (co-founder of Sun Microsystems), and John Walker (co-founder of Autodesk) to name a few. What I found fascinating, however, came from when I recently read "Outliers" by Malcom Gladwell. In this book, Gladwell contends that those people who have gained a certain level of expertise beyond that of average people have done so because:

1.) they had a certain aptitude for a particular skill,

2.) they were born on a certain date, and

3.) they acquired at least 10,000 hours of practice.

For example, professional hockey players tend to not only be naturally gifted, but most are born in the first 3 months of the year where they are given preference to early training camps, allowing them to reach the minimum 10,000 hours to become an expert at an earlier age. In the case of the computer industry, most computer freaks were born between 1953 and 1958 as well as having had early exposure to computing time. I was born in 1957. Only after reading Outliers did I understand the implications that all this had on my life (and the life of my kids).

Fast forward to the internet age, that started in about 1995. By this time, I had already been working with computer software for almost 2 decades and had written a commercial application for Landscape Architectural Computer Aided Design (Landcadd – a program that is still on the market today). I had been named "International Developer of the Year", "Colorado Small Business of the Year," and listed on the "Inc. 500." I was already well past the 10 years of experience that it normally requires to reach the 10,000-hour mark. It was only natural that I now work online. I have been doing so ever since – I am a propeller head in every sense of the word. This book is the result of what I've learned during the past 2 decades of what it takes to make money on the internet.

So, if you were to ask me why you should read this book, I'd refer you to the advice of an unknown but very wise person who said, *"Listen to your elder's advice, not because they are always right but because they have more experiences of being wrong."* I've had a lot of experience with being wrong and I can help you avoid those mistakes with your business. As Terry Pratchett said, *"Build a man a fire and he's warm for a night. Set a man on fire and he's warm for the rest of his life."* My hope is that this book will set you on fire and that you will learn from my mistakes as well as my successes.

> *A propeller-head (sometimes shortened to prophead) is jargon for someone who is exceptionally, perhaps weirdly bright or knowledgeable, especially in some technical field. The term refers to the child's beanie cap that comes with a spinning propeller sticking out of the top.*

Despite my technical background, and despite having written two other commercial software applications including a school scheduling program and a wholesale ecommerce system, this is not a technical book. It is written in everyday language to help business owners today become successful on the internet. My earlier best-selling book, "Amazon's Dirty Little Secrets" discusses how Amazon uses others to market and sell on their behalf. This book shows you how you can apply those principles to your business.

This does not mean that I think everything I tell you in this book will work for you. The fact is that one size doesn't fit all. This book is a collection of stories and methods that I and others have found to be useful for making money on the internet. But every business is different – what worked for me might not work for you...the details may change, but the system will give you a great framework.

The underlying premise is that "your opinion doesn't matter." Just because you have a Facebook or Twitter account doesn't mean that your opinion matters. Your opinions, though interesting, are irrelevant. The only thing that matters is what is working. You might like something about your website, but if a customer isn't using that feature – get rid of it. You might like a particular ad, but if no one is responding to it, you are wasting your money. This book is designed to provide you with a system so that you can only apply those marketing techniques that produce results. That is the only thing that matters.

Systems versus Goals

Scott Adams, the creator of the Dilbert comic strips, brilliantly describes the difference between goals and systems in his book, "How to Fail at Almost Everything and Still Win Big."

Adams says that goals are for losers – if your goal is to lose ten pounds, you will spend every moment until you reach your goal, feeling as if you are short of your goal. Goal-oriented people exist in a nearly permanent state of failure that they hope will only be temporary. That feeling wears on you and might even drive you out of the game. The GEARS program is designed to help you maintain your energy and to keep you excited and engaged with your efforts over the life of your business.

Think of systems and goals as very different concepts. A goal is a specific objective that you either achieve or don't achieve, sometime in the future. A system is something that you do on a regular basis that increases your odds of happiness in the long run. If you do something every day, it is a system. If you are looking to achieve it sometime in the future, it is a goal. Systems have no deadlines. On any given day, you may not be able to tell if your systems are moving you in the right direction.

Goal-oriented people exist in a state of pre-success failure all the time. If you achieve your goal, you celebrate and feel terrific, but only until you realize that you just lost the thing that gave you purpose and direction. Your options are to feel empty and useless, or to set new goals and repeat the cycle of permanent, pre-success failure. Systems people succeed every time they apply their systems. Goal oriented people are fighting discouragement at every turn; systems people are feeling good every time they apply their system. That's a huge difference in terms of maintaining your energy.

The systems versus goal model can be applied to most human endeavors: If you are dieting, losing twenty pounds is a goal, but eating right is a system. In the exercise realm, running a marathon in under four hours is a goal, but exercising daily is a system. In business, making one million dollars is a goal, but applying the steps in the GEARS program is a system. Hoping you get on the first page of Google is not a system. A system requires that it is replicable. You need definitive actionable steps that you can take. That is not to say that goals are bad, only that goals make sense when you also have a system that moves you in the direction of reaching that goal.

Successful people don't wish for success – they <u>decide</u> to do it and they have a system for accomplishing it. People who use systems instead of goals do better. If you study people who succeed, most of them follow systems, not goals. In this book, I mention Jeff Walker's PLF system. I talk about Ray Edwards' copywriting system. The reason is, systems work. That is why you should use a system like the GEARS program.

This book is meant to open you up to innovative ways of thinking about marketing and how it can help you with your online sales efforts. I expect you to challenge my assumptions, just as I frequently challenge the "way it's always been done." If you don't like what I have to say, that's okay, because your opinion doesn't count. And neither does mine. The only thing that matters is the numbers, which is why we do A/B split testing and measure everything. This will tell you if something is working. And there are clearly some things with digital marketing that aren't working, at least not for everyone. Let's start with the traditional marketing funnel.

Rethinking the Digital Marketing Funnel

Most digital marketing books talk about "funnels," and they use a diagram something like this:

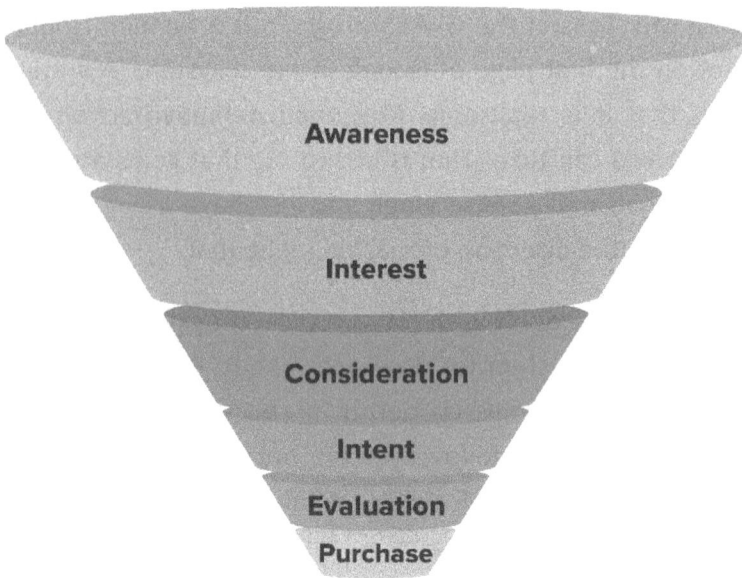

The problem with this approach is that it assumes that marketing is linear. Your customers won't all act alike, and they certainly won't follow a singular linear path down a funnel that you've predetermined. Further, the revenue portion, that which is the most important factor for any business, is the smallest piece of this system. Funnels are not bad and they are not wrong; it's just that thinking of your sales process in a linear fashion is too limiting. This book uses a different, more holistic approach. Think of it this way: in a well-developed digital marketing tool, you are building a marketing machine, not a marketing funnel. All the pieces of the machine must interact with each other. Your product, services and ideas are like the oil, and the oil must be spread across all the working parts, just like spreading the message about what you have to offer.

Gears make machines more efficient, so I use a metaphor in this book of GEARS, which makes it easy to learn and simple to remember. That way you can easily apply these principles to your business. The best systems are simple. I've made GEARS to be comprehensive, yet I've simplified it to make it easy to understand and implement.

I will also share with you the stories of what I've done and how I've helped hundreds of other companies with their online presence for the past twenty plus years. These are real-world examples, not some made up theory. And my business today continues to help others with their digital marketing, not just my own websites. If you would like to contact me as either a speaker at one of your events, or as a consultant for your online marketing, you can reach me at:

greg@gregjameson.com

or

877-924-1414 (toll free)

Chapter 1 – The Planetary Gear System

"Physicists analyze systems. Web scientists, however, can create systems."

- Tim Berners Lee
Inventor of the World Wide Web

A man, wearing a baseball cap, stood at the L'Enfant Plaza metro station in Washington DC and started to play the violin; it was a cold January morning. He played six pieces including two Bach, one Massenet, one Schubert and one Ponce for about 45 minutes. During that time, since it was rush hour, it was calculated that 1,097 people went through the station, most of them on their way to work.

Three minutes went by then a middle-aged man noticed there was musician playing. He slowed his pace and stopped for a few seconds and then hurried up to meet his schedule. A minute later, the violinist received his first dollar tip: a woman threw the money in the till and without stopping continued to walk. A few minutes later, someone leaned against the wall to listen to him, but the man looked at his watch and started to walk again. Clearly, he was late for work.

The one who paid the most attention was a 3-year-old boy. His mother tagged him along, hurried, but the kid stopped to look at the violinist. Finally, the mother pushed hard and the child continued to walk turning his head back several times. This action was repeated by several other children. All the parents, without exception, forced them to move on.

In the 45 minutes the musician played, only 7 people stopped and stayed for a while. About 20 gave him money but continued to walk their normal pace. He collected $32.17. When he finished playing and silence took over, no one noticed it. No one applauded, nor was there any recognition.

No one knew this but the violinist was Joshua Bell, one of the best musicians in the world. Bell made his Carnegie Hall debut in 1985, at age 17, with the St. Louis Symphony. He has since performed with many of the world's major orchestras and conductors. Bell's instrument is a 300-year-old Stradivarius violin called the Gibson ex Huberman, which was made in 1713 during what is known as Antonio Stradivari's "Golden Era." It is worth 3.5 million dollars.

Two days before his playing in the subway, Joshua Bell sold out at a theater in Boston and the seats average $100.

This is a real story. Joshua Bell playing incognito in the metro station was organized by the Washington Post as part of a social experiment.

Online marketing is much like the Joshua Bell experiment. A website may be listed on the first page of Google and be seen by over one thousand viewers. Perhaps seven of those viewers will actually click on the link and visit the site. The odds of getting visitors to your website when no one knows who you are, is extremely low. Whether you are in front of a thousand people at a subway station, or you are listed on the first page of Google, it is not enough. You need a way for people to know you. What if others had told their friends that there would be a free concert by a world-famous musician on that day? This experiment was repeated a few years later, and this time they advertised the fact that Joshua Bell would be playing in the subway station. The result was thousands of people packed in to hear him play. What if others recommended your site to their friends and told them who you were? You need a system and GEARS is that system.

The acronym GEARS used in this book is not simply a word that makes it easy to learn how to "G.E.A.R. up for online Success". It is meant to be a visual tool that makes it easy to remember. As such, I've constructed this diagram of a planetary gear system:

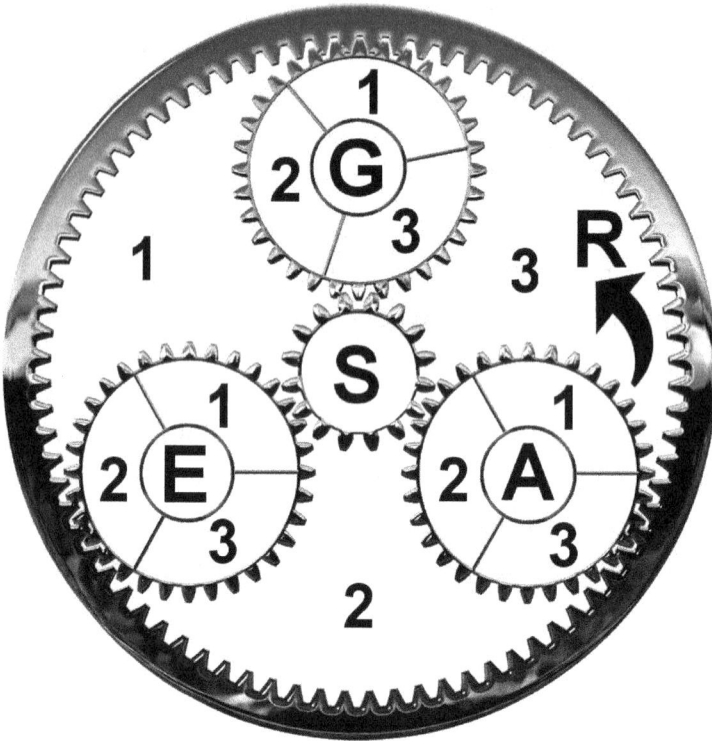

The parts of this gear system are as follows:

The center gear is called a "sun" gear. This is what makes everything else work, and I'll discuss the importance of this gear in the section on "**Strategy**".

The three gears that circle the sun gear are the "planet gears." The gears, "G, E, and A" comprise the primary methods used to develop a following and how to market your online business.

They stand for "**G**enerate interest", "**E**mpower influencers", and "**A**mplify your message". Each is discussed in the appropriate sections later in this book, with three main components (chapters) for each.

The outer gear is called a "ring gear." This gear encircles all the other gears. We'll discuss this in the section on "**R**esults." The ring gear is also divided into three chapters: Revenues, Review & Repeat, and Research.

To recap, GEARS stands for:

G – Generate Interest

E – Empower influencers

A – Amplify your message

R – Results

S - Strategy

The teeth on each gear represent a single action you must take. As you can see in the sidebar, it takes about 80 actions before you see your first result. The actions must be more-or-less equally distributed across the various gears. Putting all your efforts into a single action like SEO (Search Engine Optimization) won't work. In other words, putting up a website, then running a single ad is not enough.

For the geeks out there, here is how you calculate the number of actions in this system to complete a single turn or result:

For convenience, let's denote R, S, and P as the number of teeth on the gears

R   Number of teeth in ring gear

S   Number of teeth in sun (middle) gear

P   Number of teeth in planet gears

The first requirement for a planetary gear to work, is that all the teeth have the same pitch, or tooth spacing. This ensures that the teeth mesh.

The second requirement is:

$R = 2 \times P + S$

That is to say, the number of teeth in the ring gear is equal to the number of teeth in the middle sun gear plus twice the number of teeth in the planet gears.

In the gear diagram I showed previously, this would be

$80 = 2 \times 32 + 16$

Think of each tooth in the gears as an action that we must take to complete one-gear cycle. What this means in our sample diagram is that we must take 80 actions to achieve the desired results. That is a lot of work. **Eighty actions before you see your first sale.**

The reason why this is so important is that 80 to 97% of ecommerce websites fail! This number is so high because most ecommerce sites do not have a proven method in place to ensure their success. Rather than running their business like a well-oiled machine, they are continuously hoping to discover the one thing that will make them succeed online, and they never figure it out.

According to Practical Ecommerce (Nov. 7, 2014), 80% of ecommerce websites fail. Other studies put this figure as high as 97%, including Forrester, a leading web research firm, most of whom blame interface design as the reason for failure. As you'll see in this book, the cause is often not something as simple as web design.

You may not want to hear this, but the truth is that running an online business is not a get-rich quick scheme. In fact, it is hard. It's often harder than a physical brick and mortar business because people can't see you or your products. They are relying on trust, which is often extremely difficult to achieve in today's world of cyber security issues. If you are going to have an online business today (and I contend that all businesses today are at least partially online businesses), then you are going to have to work it just like any other business. My friend Michael Neil says, "if you are struggling to earn money online, quit focusing on the $$$ and focus on helping others, magic will happen." The point is, you cannot simply put up a website and hope that it works like magic. It won't. By applying the GEARS method, you can drastically improve your chances.

One of the things you will quickly figure out as you read this book is that you must have multiple income streams. Having an online store where all you do is offer products for sale is a large part of why many ecommerce websites fail. You need multiple ways of generating income on your site. In my book, Amazon's Dirty Little Secrets, I show you the numerous ways that Amazon makes money including advertising, Amazon Web Services, a membership program (Prime), content (both Kindle content and video/TV content), co-branded credit cards, and third-party sellers. Ecommerce is only one of their revenue streams, and perhaps their least profitable. Even Amazon, if all they did was to sell retail products, would not be profitable, and you won't be either.

Another thing you will discover in this book is that you must own your client list. Yes, it's great to have a large social media following. I use social media, especially Facebook, extensively in the methods I'm going to share with you. But ultimately, you want those people on your email list. Relying on social media is like living in a rented apartment – you don't own the prospect. Facebook, LinkedIn, Twitter, or whoever can change the rules on you overnight or delete your account. Only by moving people off your social media accounts and onto your own list will enable you to control your own destiny. Having 1,000 or 100,000 followers on social media is not the same as having an email list of the same size. Most of the money I derive from the GEARS method ends up coming from my own email list. As you read through this book, I encourage you to think of how you can continue to grow your own list.

So, there you have it – what it takes to be successful online. You must have a passion for what you are doing with the realization that you are going to have to continuously take actions, have multiple income streams, create a customer email list, and have a proven method to implement. This book is that method. Let's get started!

G: Generate Interest

"If dogs don't like your dog food, the packaging doesn't matter."

- Stephen Denny
Competitive Strategy & Marketing Consultant

FOREWORD by Armand Morin

Everyday thousands of people start their journey to create their dream and destiny by being their own boss and starting their own business. More and more of those people choose the Internet as their vehicle to build and promote their products and services. And, as we all know, a large percentage of those people end up failing and not knowing why.

After training thousands upon thousands of people from all over the world, I can tell you in two simply words why their failed... a system. They didn't have a duplicable system that has been time-tested and proven to work. Just like every McDonald's is the same, so are the many aspects of running a business online and offline.

This is precisely the reason you are reading this book right now. You need a system, but not just any system a system that works.

What makes Greg's book different is the approach he takes.

What I love about it is that he's not trying to get you to build one huge mega site and put all your eggs into one basket. When you look at his scouting site, it's not making a fortune by itself but its generating residual income month after month.

Years ago, I taught a group of people how to generate income through Google's Adsense program. What they were shocked was that I didn't have just one site earning me income, I had a network of sites all earning me $300-$500 each per month.

Where if one went down or stopped working, it wasn't the end, because I had hundreds of sites doing the same thing. This is a different way of thinking and quite honestly a more reliable way for many people.

But it's not just income.

The Internet relies on a well-balanced program of traffic, copy, marketing and conversion strategies. When you really think about it, it's kind of like the legs on a table if one isn't there the whole table falls over.

As an example... you could have the greatest website and product in the world, but if no one sees it and you have no website visitors no one is going purchase anything from you.

Another example... if your words are not compelling and reach out to the reader in way to make them want your product or service, then again... no one will buy anything.

Another example... many people think you just need to put up a website and people will find you. Not true by any remote means. You need a complete marketing strategy to tell the world what you have.

One last example... if your visitors come to your site and your site does not sell, meaning it does not convert, then all the traffic in the world will not help you AND no one will buy

This all might sound confusing to you but it's much easier than it sounds when you have someone guiding you. And more importantly, you can even outsource some of this work to others for literally a few pennies on the dollar.

As you can see, it's all part of system.

Greg's system he outlines in The Influencer Effect will allow you to utilize these methods to gain other's credibility to help you market your products and services.

I've seen Greg's presentation on this and he knows what he's talking about. Read each word carefully and implement The Influencer Effect into your business today!

Armand Morin

http://ArmandMorin.com

Chapter 2 – Give Something Away

"You can earn attention by creating something interesting and valuable and then publishing it online for free."

- David Meerman Scott
Marketing Strategist & Author

This book is supposed to be about online success and making money on the internet, so why is the very first thing addressed is talking about giving something away for free? Everything in our economy is moving towards being free. It used to cost thousands of dollars to build a website, but today you can do it for (almost) free using programs like Wix, Weebly, Squarespace, and even WordPress. This has put many website designers out of business. Medical advice, legal advice, and "how-to" information on every profession can be found for free on the internet. Do you think you are immune because you sell physical products instead of information? Think again. With 3D printing technology, everything we know can be reduced to a digital file and given away for free. As I'm writing this, I went to Thingverse.com, a site where you can download 3D printer files, and the featured item for the day was a complete engine for a Chevy Camaro that you could "print" yourself. How can you possibly make money in a free economy?

The reality is that having a website does not mean that anyone will come to it, much less buy anything from you. That is like thinking that having a business card or company brochure will generate interest in your business. You need something much more compelling than that. You have to get people interested in what you have to offer, and the single best way to do this is to give something away. People love getting stuff for free, whether you give them a sample product or enter them in a drawing for a larger prize. You might even give them a "gift certificate" for a specified amount. Note: don't call it a coupon. Call it a gift certificate. This makes the potential customer feel more important.

Most marketers will tell you to create a "lead magnet" or "ethical bribe" like an eBook or whitepaper that is strong enough that visitors will give you their email address. While this is better than simply having a form that says, "join my email list," I contend that this is not enough. This is old school thinking. People used to respond to a one-page sales letter where you "gave away your best stuff," and then you would attempt to continuously upsell the person to buy more and more information from you. This no longer works. Adding more and more training courses, utilities, and charts to bump up the perceived value of an offering may actually turn people off. Look, people are not stupid. They know real value when they see it, and you need to provide that value.

You need to give them something so valuable that they will go out and tell all their friends about it and drive traffic to your website for you! This is key – *what you offer must be valuable enough that visitors will not only gladly give you their email address, but will want to share what you have with everyone*

they know. And it doesn't have to be worth $1,000 or even $100, it just need to be something that they want. One way to accomplish this, if you have a WordPress website, is to use a plugin like "wpLike2Get." This requires that a visitor share your page on social media before they can access your free giveaway. You could also use "Opt-In Panda." Opt-In Panda locks a portion of content on a webpage by hiding it and asks the visitor to enter one's email address (opt-in) to unlock your content. This gives visitors a reason to subscribe right now in return to instant access to your valuable content (e.g. downloads, discounts, videos and so on).

Let me tell you about my first experience with a free product and how I stumbled across this principle quite by accident.

I was involved in the Boy Scouts of America for over 25 years. While serving as Scoutmaster, each year we would train the new boys who would be leading the troop for the next twelve months. They would go through a day-long course called JLT – Junior Leadership Training. At the end of the day, I wanted to award each of them with a certificate indicating that they had completed the course. Now, being the gear-head that I am, I didn't want to create a bunch of individual certificates, I wanted to create a single certificate and then just type in each of their names to generate individual certificates for each of them. I wrote a little program that allowed me to do just that.

It worked well enough for me, so I decided to share this with some of the other Scoutmasters I knew, as I thought it would benefit them as well. I emailed about a dozen of my friends and simply said, "if you find this useful for your troop, let me know what you think of it and how I can improve it." These scoutmasters are what I later came to learn were "micro-influencers," but I hadn't heard of that term at the time.

By the very next morning, I had started to get email from all over the world: South America, Asia, Africa, and Europe! They all said something like "Wow! Thanks for creating this. This is going to save me a ton of time. I'm sharing it with other members of my local council." What started out as a friendly gesture went viral overnight.

Clearly, I was on to something, so I made a few minor improvements and offered the ability to create certificates not only for JLT, but for any scout-related activity, whether you were an adult volunteer, a cub scout crossing over into Boy Scouts, earning a new rank, or anything that deserved recognition. Basically, the way this worked was: you chose a certificate orientation, either vertical (portrait mode), or horizontal (landscape mode). Then you selected a background image or border. Next you would choose a "seal" and if desired, a "ribbon." Finally, you would enter in the text and select the fonts for each line of text. The program would dynamically generate a PDF file that could be printed out on standard 8.5" x 11" paper. However, before anyone could print the certificate, a preview would be shown to them with a message that said, "Cool certificate! If you would like to download and print this, please enter your email below."

This became so popular that I was sure I was going to get in trouble with the Boy Scouts. They are very concerned about their trademarks and I thought I would get a phone call any day.

Instead, what happened was that they featured me on their blog! This increased the visibility even more. Many of the email addresses that came in from filling out my form were from executives at the Boy Scouts of America – they were using the program themselves!

This certificate maker is still active. I do very little to maintain or update the program – it works on auto-pilot. And to this day, I still get an average of 30 emails a day of people creating new certificates. Think about that, 30 emails times 30 days in a month is almost 1,000 new email addresses I collect every month that I can now market to with other products and services. This isn't some eBook or training course with an artificial value of hundreds or thousands of dollars – it is a simple product that visitors find compelling enough to share with their friends without even being asked to.

You can access the certificate wizard from the home page of CyberbaseTradingPost.com.

Since that turned out so well, I thought, what else can I share with scouters around the world that they will find valuable? I tried a few things – and not all of them worked. For example, I tried creating a directory of resources that people could add to themselves in order that people could search on things like "best places to camp in a certain area," or "where to get supplies for a Blue & Gold banquet." This did not take off. But two other things that did work reasonably well were my "Letter of Congratulations to new Eagle Scouts" and my "Instructions for an "Indoor Campfire."

The Eagle Scout congratulations letter is still available for download. This is the story of five young men who were trapped inside of Columbine High School during the time of the nation's worst school shooting in history. Between them, they saved the lives of hundreds of their fellow students. All five of these young men were Eagle Scouts and were awarded the Medal of Honor by the Boy Scouts of America for their bravery and heroism. It is a legacy that today's Eagle Scouts can seek to live up to.

It was not necessary to enter an email to download this letter. Anyone could print it and use it as is. If they wanted me to print the letter, sign it, and send it to the new Eagle Scout, I would be happy to do so at no charge.

The indoor campfire was something that came about as a result of participating in numerous crossover or bridging ceremonies where cub scouts would become Boy Scouts. These ceremonies were often done in January in Colorado. This is a time when it was cold and snowing outside. Now as Boy Scouts, we would camp twelve months of the year, including in the snow, but this did not make for a very good ceremony with young cub scouts and their families. These were usually held in a school gymnasium or church. But we wanted to have a campfire! So, I spent a lot of time trying to develop a realistic looking fake campfire. It took multiple attempts and it evolved over time, but eventually I created a fake campfire that was realistic enough that we actually had the fire department called in on several events. The dancing silk flame, the fog machine "smoke," and the ambient sounds of a crackling fire all contributed to make this a multi-sensory experience that looked like a real fire.

I made a video of the campfire and posted instructions on Cyberbase Trading Post on how to assemble such a campfire yourself. Again, you didn't need to enter an email to have access to this, it was just posted for informational purposes, although the components that made up the campfire were available for sale on my site. We'll talk more about this in the next chapter. And like the certificate wizard, the fake campfire instructions have been viewed thousands of times on YouTube and shared often without ever having asked anyone to do so.

Now you might be saying, "That's great. You stumbled upon making a certificate wizard for your site, but my company is different." If eBooks, white papers, and online courses don't work effectively, what can I give away that is shareable by others?" Believe me, I've struggled with this as much as anyone. My primary business is not Cyberbase Trading Post, it is WebStores Ltd, a company that helps others with their online marketing and digital advertising. Over the years, we've had to adapt from being an ecommerce web design firm, to offering value in other ways. I could give away my time, but that isn't very shareable. You need something that people talk about and are excited to share.

One thing that almost everyone can give away that is shareable is webinars – basically 30 to 90 minutes of your time where you provide valuable content in a live setting. The great thing about webinars is that you can record them and use them over and over. This makes them highly shareable, assuming you are providing great content. You can interact with your attendees, and you don't even have to have very many attendees who are on "live" with you. Some people charge for webinars, but I recommend giving them away as a lead magnet. Most webinars I've attended will try to sell you something, often something very expensive, as the end as part of their "special offer." If you don't buy, then you are dropped. If that works for you, fine, but it is not why I would use a webinar – I recommend doing webinars for the sole purpose of getting someone's email address and adding them to your list. Once they are on your list, you will be able to sell them something in the future. In fact, I recommend that your "special offer" at the end of your webinar is another freebie: specifically, an infographic of what you've just covered. An infographic is basically a graphical way of portraying information, such as a menu, a step-by-step guide, a formula, or method that makes your concept easy to understand. The infographic should be a high-resolution jpg or pdf file that can be printed out at poster size and hung on the prospects' wall.

I have developed such an infographic that accompanies this book. Visit

GregJameson.com/GEARS

and I will send you this infographic as a gift for reading my book. If you would like to learn more about conducting webinars, my colleague, Lewis Howes, a New York Times Best-Selling author and lifestyle entrepreneur who recently appeared on the Ellen Show, is the master of all things related to webinars. Check out his site at LewisHowes.com.

I mention webinars multiple times in this book. There are multiple ways of creating webinars, but I another have free gift for you:

Visit bit.ly/foreverwebinar to sign up for a "Forever Free" webinar hosting platform.

Another one of my colleagues, Jeff Walker, says that when you are launching a product or service, you don't need a list. Instead you need a launch in order to build a list. This may seem counter-intuitive, but he is absolutely correct. I didn't have a list when I released the Certificate Wizard. You don't need a list to do a webinar. You can share it on social media, and if others find it valuable, they will share it for you and you can then grow your list. At this stage, you are simply trying to establish the "know, like and trust" factor. And when you give away something that has enough value to be shareable, your email list will grow.

I should tell you a little more about Jeff Walker's concept for launching a product or service and how he uses this as a means to build your list. He calls his program PLF or the "Product Launch Formula" and basically it works like this: Instead of using an old school long sales letter, you create a "sideways sales letter," turning that sales copy into a series of 4 or more emails where you keep giving them a video or other content along the way. You don't ask for the sale until at least the fourth email. If what you are selling is digital information, you have to establish a know, like, and trust factor before someone will purchase from you. For example, I could create a series of five videos about the GEARS methods – one video for each letter. On the

35

fifth video, you will have received enough free information that you might be willing to buy my products and services. Even if you don't buy anything, this can be a good way for me to grow my email list for future sales.

Here's another way to help launch your product or service: use www.Thunderclap.it. This site is the first-ever platform that helps people be heard by saying something together at the same time. It allows a single message to be mass-shared, flash mob-style, so it rises above the noise of your social networks. By boosting the signal at the same time, Thunderclap helps a single person create action like never before. Thunderclap didn't exist when I launched the certificate wizard, but I did use when I launched my previous book, helping reach almost two million people in a single day. The result was that it hit number one on Amazon.

Recently, I participated in the re-launch of a book that had been on the market for years. Its sales had flattened, so the author, Stephanie Frank, with the help of her coach Linda Stirling, created a campaign to launch the book a second time. They created a private Facebook group to post about what they were doing, including asking everyone in the group to participate in a thunderclap campaign, followed by buying the book and writing a review about it. The Thunderclap campaign ended up reaching over three million people. Within two days, the book became a number one international best-seller in multiple categories. Imagine how this can help you if you are simply launching a free product or announcing a webinar.

I have a customer who makes gourmet popcorn. He talked about giving away free samples of his popcorn online, but decided against it as he was concerned about shipping costs. That is understandable. What about entering people into a drawing to get a gift box containing multiple flavors of his popcorn? Or, using the webinar concept, he could create a webinar on how someone could make their own gifts using popcorn: snowmen made of popcorn balls including decorating tips. Then he could give them an infographic with the instructions. Now he has them on his list and he can sell them popcorn in the future.

Which leads us to the question, what can your company give away as a lead magnet that would be so compelling that people would want to share it with their family and friends? If you run a travel agency, perhaps you could enter people into a drawing for a free cruise. If you have a restaurant, give away a free meal. A Christmas store? How about a free ornament? A friend of

> *I've heard people refer to your free product as an IFO – Irresistible Free Offer. For this to work, your IFO should be widely desired and easy to reproduce.*

mine makes Native American Flutes, a beautiful instrument handcrafted out of wood that costs hundreds of dollars. The simple thing would be to give away something digital, such as sheet music and tablature to a particular song, or even a lesson on how to play the native American Flute. Instead, each month he "raffles" off one of his flutes and announces it in his newsletter as to who the lucky winner is. Remember, don't be cheap or bashful – the idea is to give something away that is so compelling that people will want to share it. It doesn't have to be your own product either – find a partner who will donate a give-away as part of a joint marketing effort. It helps if it is related to your business, but it doesn't have to be. For example, a limousine service doesn't have to give away limo rides. They might give away a new smart phone (with your app pre-loaded on it of course!). The point is, your free offer should not just be considered "bait." It should be something of value so that others will want to share it, not just claim it because it is free.

I have a friend whose young daughter proudly showed him a page in a coloring book that she had scribbled on and said, "Daddy, look what I made for you!" He replied, "That's nice Nikki, but try to stay within the lines. Here, try again." So, Nikki colored a new page and showed it to her dad. He said again, "That's nice Nikki, but I told you to stay within the lines. Try again." This went on for a few times and my friend was getting frustrated. So was his daughter – she finally said "Daddy, what lines?"

When it comes to determining what you can give away, don't just think outside the lines. Question the very existence of the lines themselves. Keep experimenting until you discover your own "certificate wizard."

Chapter 3 – Get Upsells

"Do you want fries with that?"

- McDonalds Restaurants

Only after you've built a relationship with your visitor by giving them something of value, as discussed in the previous chapter, are you ready to sell them something. This can be done on the first visit, but remember the rule of seven – it usually takes at least seven "touches" with a prospect before they buy. Therefore, be gentle with the first attempt at trying to close a sale. Unless you are the type that would ask someone to marry you on the first date (like my cousin did!), I recommend that you simply test the waters.

The best way to do this is to upsell what you offered for free. In my case, at the end of the process of creating a free certificate, I provide the visitor with an opportunity to purchase a frame to go with the certificate. This is actually a very valuable service. You see, most frames are made for 8x10 photos, not 8 ½" x 11" paper that you print out from your computer. Standard photo frames are too small. Plus, they are boring! Who wants to put a fun, whimsical certificate in a black plastic frame? Even a serious certificate of accomplishment for scouting looks better in a wooden frame, especially if it has been designed with a scouting theme and can be customized. I had some frames made up that are laser-engraved with different themes: a leader themed frame, a pinewood derby themed frame, a camping themed frame, a hiking themed frame, etc. You get the idea. These are nice wood frames which are designed specifically to hold a certificate printed on a standard sheet of paper. They are ordered as one-offs and are drop-shipped directly from the manufacturer with my name on it. Of course, the frames can be customized with a date, name and event if desired, and they can be ordered at any time. It makes sense to ask for the upsell as soon as someone has finished printing their certificate.

One thing I discovered was that there are some people who were taking advantage of the free service, creating as many as 20 or 30 certificates at once. I didn't really care, but this started putting a burden on the server resources, which was costing me money. I needed to deflect those costs, so I put a "Donate Now" button on the site. Surprisingly, people do donate – I've received donations for as much as $75. Clearly it would be possible for someone to go and purchase a nice custom certificate made for much less than that, but they feel like they are helping a cause.

Another thing I added later was a feature that I called a "Premium Certificate." If you wanted to print more than ten certificates in a twenty-four-hour period, I decided to charge them. The cost would be minimal. In fact $6.97 would give you unlimited certificates for an entire month. There were other features added to the premium certificates as well. One could upload their own background designs, they could save their certificate layouts and come back and print them at a later time (great if you run out of ink or just want to save your design), and add multiple names in order to print multiple copies of the same certificate. The idea was to add lots of value at a

> *I use a plugin called Paid Memberships Pro to administer the Premium Certificate program.*

price that anyone could afford. Like Amazon with their Prime membership program however, I decided to make this a continuity program. That is, the premium certificates became a membership program that would automatically bill the customer every month. They could opt-out whenever they wanted, but if they don't opt-out, their credit card gets automatically charged each month for $6.97. Every serious ecommerce website needs some type of membership program.

The best upsell product I ever had was a native American hand-beaded award arrow. I met an old Navajo named Yellowhorse at the Denver March Pow wow one year whose wife made the beautiful arrows with a hand-chipped stone arrowhead, turkey feather fletching, and wrapped them in beadwork and rabbit fur. I bought one from him for $10 and brought it home. My wife said, *"Can you get more of these? They would sell on Cyberbase."* So, I went back and asked Yellowhorse if I could buy them from him in bulk. *"Sure, if you buy 20 of them. But the best I can sell them to you is for $6 apiece."* I tried hard not to smile, *"OK, you got a deal."*

I sold all of them in a few days for $24 each – a 4 times markup. They were being used by cub scout leaders as awards for when boys crossed over from Cub Scouts into Boy Scouts who had earned their Arrow of Light award. I called Yellowhorse (he lived in a remote part of the reservation and didn't have email), and asked him if I could buy more. He gladly shipped them to me for the same price.

Of course, I had to figure out how to ship these to my customers. But as it turns out, the post office makes a priority mail box that is a three-inch triangular shaped box which is thirty six inches long. Perfect! These boxes could easily ship one to six arrows, almost as if they were designed to do so. The boxes were free and the shipping cost only about seven dollars.

After a couple of years, Yellowhorse raised the price on me to $8. It was no big deal, I just raised my price to $32 and they kept selling. Anytime you can charge four times your buying price, you can make a lot of money. I did some research and found that the only competing product was being sold in tourist shops with about one-third the amount of beadwork and the arrows were only about twenty eight inches long instead of thirty three inches like Yellowhorse's arrows were. They were being sold for $95. I knew I had a good deal and was able to sell these at a low cost while making good money. In fact, the arrows were so impressive that I would get unsolicited feedback from customers thanking me for providing these – testimonials are huge as I'll discuss in a later chapter.

One year, Yellowhorse brought some arrows to the Denver March Pow wow that were fully beaded with only a little bit of the shaft showing around the rabbit fur. *"The best I can sell these to you is for $12 because of the amount of beadwork on* them," he explained. *"OK, I'll take them all,"* I said. I sold those for $50 each and they were gone almost immediately. People were buying them not only for Cub Scouts, but as gifts for Eagle Scouts and the Order of the Arrow.

Sadly, Yellowhorse informed me that the cost of beads had gone up and that his wife and daughter could no longer keep up. They would no longer be making arrows. I tried to plead with him and told him that I would pay the increased price, but he said they were done. I lost my supplier and have never found a replacement that was as good, regardless of price. It was great while it lasted, and I'd love to sell award arrows again.

In the previous chapter, I also talked about my instructions for making a fake campfire. Guess where you can buy all the components to actually make that fake campfire? You got it, right there on my website. I also provide an mp3 digital download of a crackling fire audio loop, but I sell the silk flame, the lights, and the fog machine. Mind you, this is not a high-pressure sales tactic, just a convenience for people who are interested.

When I first started selling the components to make the fake fire, I found the supplies on eBay. I would buy them from whoever was selling them the cheapest, have them sent to me, and I would re-package the items and ship them to my customer. One supplier noticed that I was buying a lot of the same thing and contacted me. I told him what I was doing and he suggested that I order directly from him rather than through eBay. The price would be better and he would drop ship them for me, with my name and address on the package. I was not aware of drop shipping at the time, but it seemed like the perfect solution, and for a while it worked great. Eventually, though, he too went out of business and I lost another supplier. I decided that I should reach out directly to the manufacturer, Chauvet, and sign up as a reseller for them. Apparently, I wasn't a big enough deal to them as I was only selling silk flames and fog machines. They were in the business of selling to DJ's and night clubs and wanted resellers that would carry their full line of products including laser-light and disco balls. They suggested I buy through a distributor rather than direct.

I tried some alternatives, including the cheap plastic "Halloween cauldrons," but the quality was so poor that I ended up with too many returns. I had to find another Chauvet distributor as I didn't have another choice.

What I really wanted to do was to go to China and have the pieces made for me to my specifications. Then everything could be packaged as a single unit and sold as a "fake campfire kit." The problem was, even though I was able to sell a few of these each month, I knew the volume wasn't high enough to justify a custom product. Private labeling would have been ideal if there were no minimum volumes, but I couldn't find anyone to do this. Then the Chauvet silk flames started showing up on Amazon at a price less than I could buy them from a distributor.

Rather than completely throw in the towel, I became an affiliate for Amazon and now offer the parts of the fake campfire as an affiliate link. But like the award arrows, I'd still like to sell my own product, and this is an important point for online stores. If possible, have your upsell products be something that you make and control yourself. Just like you want to own your customer list and not be "renting" followers from some social media platform, you want your upsell products to be something that you control.

The concept of upselling after giving away a free, but valuable product, is used by most software developers, especially WordPress plugins. You can download the plugin or software and use it, but extended functionality will cost you some money. The most successful ones using this approach will not charge customers a lot of money for the first upsell. The idea is to get them comfortable spending money with you. After they have purchased a small ticket item, you may offer them a second upsell that costs more.

I've seen people try to upsell customers on one thing after another as they move through their sales funnel. I do not believe this is being honest and recommend against it. Upsell them once with a small ticket item, then offer a second upsell for a larger ticket item. You can give them options on the second upsell, such as 1 seat versus 5 seats versus unlimited seats, but don't first try to upsell them and then try to down sell them. That is an insult and makes you look desperate.

The purpose of upsell products is not to sell the customer everything you have, nor is it too move them to the end of your sales funnel. The purpose is to simply make them your customer instead of a visitor. Most ecommerce sites miss this concept. They put up a webstore, and expect that people will just start buying from them. It doesn't work that way. You must move them through the process as I've described. My friend and colleague, Brian G. Johnson, refers to this in his book as a "Trust Funnel." You need a trust funnel to get people to start buying from you. Give them a free and valuable product, then create an upsell or two to entice them to purchase from you.

Once they have purchased from you, if you treat them well and you earn their trust, they will then be more willing to continue to buy things from you in the future. At that point, you can start to send them offers for special sales and drive them to your traditional ecommerce store where they can add lots of things to their shopping cart. Of course, to do that you'll need to keep them coming back to your website, which is what I talk about in the next chapter.

Chapter 4 – Give Them a Reason to Come Back

"It's much easier to double your business by doubling your conversion rate than by doubling your traffic."

- Jeff Eisenberg
CEO BuyerLegends.com

Imagine if every time you visited Facebook that you were presented with the exact same information. All of your friend's posts were the same – the site never changed. It's pretty likely that you would stop going back to Facebook every day.

Your site is no different. If any site is not updated on a regular basis, it is considered stagnant. This is one of the reasons why Google constantly changes their search results algorithm. They want their site to be different and relative to their visitors based on current events. That is why the current Google search results include a "freshness" variable to determine how frequently a site is updated. The more frequently you update your site, the more likely that visitors will return to your site and the more value they will get out of it when they do visit.

Updating your website as frequently as Facebook does, of course, isn't realistic, as there are so many people contributing to that site. What you need to do is figure out a way that you can either automate the process of updating your site or get others to contribute to your site. This does not mean that you don't also need to update your site yourself. And you will need to do so regularly (at least weekly). The content you create must be valuable enough that it will get your visitors to return to your site over and over again because they don't want to miss anything! Remember how I said that you were going to have to work your website just like any other business? Well, this content creation on an on-going basis is a big part of that. I said it at the beginning of this book, but it bears repeating: you can't just put up a website and magically expect that people are going to start buying from you.

Here's another way of looking at this – think of a physical store. If you own a brick and mortar shop, you realize that your inventory changes constantly and that you must change your point-of-sale displays to match the time of the year, current holidays and any sales you are having. You are constantly changing your brick and mortar store and you must constantly be changing your website. It's all about merchandising and there are no exceptions.

Amazon is once again our example to follow. Every time you visit Amazon they are promoting new products, based upon past buying and search history. Just like Facebook, what they display on their home page is different for every customer. And it is all about the customer, not about them. Don't make the mistake of putting "About Us" content on your home page. If you have any sentences that begin with "I or we or our," remove those and put them elsewhere on your site. The customer wants to know about what's in it for him, not about you.

More importantly, Amazon doesn't just sit around and wait for you to come back. Amazon encourages you to visit them by sending you emails. We'll talk more about that in a later chapter. For now, recognize that you need to not only update your website on a continual basis, but that you need to encourage your customers to keep coming back. This is true whether you are selling products on your website or not, even an information, brochure-type site needs to do this or they will quickly fail. I realize that your company is not Amazon any more than it is Facebook, but there are some things that even a small company can do to keep its site fresh.

Here's what I do for Cyberbase Trading Post: I write a new blog post approximately once a week on a topic that is of interest to scouts and scout leaders. If you don't like writing blog posts, you should create audio or video blogs, but you need to generate content – and lots of it. In my case, I do all of these, making videos with scoutmaster minutes (teachable moments), and I give them to my visitors in written form as well. I also discuss leadership skills, camping and hiking tips, and news related to scouting. The articles don't have to be long, but they do need to be relevant and consistent.

This is still not enough content to make my site be or look different every day, so I supplement this with some automated blog posts. I use a WordPress plugin called "Amabot" that allows me to enter my Amazon affiliate id and specific search terms, then how many blog posts and the frequency that I want these automated posts to appear. For example, I can enter in "Boy Scouts" from the Amazon category of "Outdoor Gear" and have it post information about products that meet those search criteria on an hourly or daily basis. The program grabs the product description and photo from Amazon, inserts my affiliate link, and generates the blog posts for me.

On my home page, I display the snippets from the last three blog posts, so the content is different every day, even though I am only writing something myself once every week or two. I also have a newsletter that is auto-generated from my blog posts. I formatted the newsletter only once using a plugin called "MailPoet" to create a template. These newsletters are triggered based upon my blog posts, not the automated ones, so they go out weekly rather than daily. I'll talk more about staying in contact with your customers in a later chapter, but the point is that you only have to write something once, then re-purpose it with automated techniques. The technology itself is not what is important. What's important is the concept of automating as much as possible, regardless of where the technology takes us in the future.

The other way to make your site be constantly updated is to follow the lead of sites like Facebook, YouTube, Wikipedia, eBay and Amazon – let your customers contribute to the site. In the case of Cyberbase Trading Post, I do this by providing a directory listing. The directory contains all things related to scouting: campgrounds, entertainers, craft supplies, fundraising opportunities, etc. Visitors can add to the directory and share their favorite resources with other scouts including photos and a description. The listing must be approved, which keeps out inappropriate items from appearing on the site. Once a directory listing is approved, other scouts and scouters can "vote" on the listing with a one to five-star rating and leave their own feedback. This is highly interactive and keeps the visitors engaged and coming back. The plugin used to accomplish this is called "Sabai directory."

The idea here is really two-fold: Generate lots of relevant content that is interesting enough to make your visitors want to come back, then provide the opportunity for them to interact with you (or your other visitors). You want to start a conversation with your customers. You can make this happen by allowing them to post comments on your blog posts or creating a "forum" inside your membership area. But remember, interaction is key and will help you sell more of what you are offering, whether it is a product or a service. Communicating with your customers will encourage them to keep coming back.

One way to get them to come back is to simply celebrate your customers. This could be via a blog post, by highlighting a "customer of the week." Dunkin Donuts did this as part of a Facebook cover photo campaign. You can bet that anyone who was selected, shared this with their friends!

You could also entice them to come back. For example, what if you created a loyalty program for your website that was similar to a "frequent flyer" program? Instead of buying products, all the customer had to do was show up, read a blog post, and then comment on the post or share it on social media. This would give them a reason to come back to your site, since they would be earning points that could be redeemed for something of value. I know of only one WordPress plugin that can be used for creating these types of incentives, called "Gratisfaction." You can get it at

http://bit.ly/rewardplatform.

Gratisfaction allows you to reward your customers for a range of actions they may take including:

- Referrals: Reward your customers for bringing in referrals that generate new sales for your business.
- Subscribing to your Newsletter: Increase subscriptions by rewarding participants for sign ups.
- Account signups: Reward visitors with points for registering an account.

- Social shares: Give participants points or instant rewards for spreading your store's message to the public on your behalf.
- Social media actions: Give participants points or instant rewards for interacting with your store's web presence such as following you on Twitter, visiting your Facebook Page, tweeting or retweeting posts, watching your YouTube video, and so on.
- And, of course, purchases: Reward loyalty points to your customers for purchases on your WooCommerce store.

Having such a system would encourage loyal followers to promote your content to their friends and followers, becoming an influencer for your brand, which we discuss in detail in the next section.

E: Empower Influencers

"People do not buy goods and services. They buy relations, stories and magic."

- Seth Godin
Best-Selling author, Entrepreneur and Marketer

FOREWORD by Steve Olsher

Have you heard of Stacy Tuschl, JJ Flizanes or Nicole Holland? How about Jordan Harbinger or Michael O'Neal? If you have, then you already know that these amazing women and men, and hundreds of others just like them, are the "Oprahs", "Larry Kings" and "Howard Sterns" of today who are able to reach thousands upon thousands of people with simply the push of a button. If you haven't, then please pay close attention to what you're about to read.

Just a few short years ago, if you wanted to reach the masses with your mission and message, you had two choices:

• Hire an expensive PR firm and hope to land a coveted appearance on The Today Show, Good Morning America, Oprah or similar programs.
Or,
• Buy expensive radio or television commercials, newspaper or magazine ads or spend a fortune on direct mail campaigns.

For most, these options were far too cost prohibitive. And, for those who could afford the inordinate expense, if they were LUCKY, a miniscule fraction of the people who were exposed to their message would have a meaningful interest in their teachings or offerings.

Fortunately, times have changed and, today, there are hundreds of 'Oprahs'. They're Influencers... and, if you haven't received the memo yet, Influencer marketing is the fastest growing, visibility generating medium on the face of the planet.

People are becoming immune to traditional advertisements and are sometimes even actively ignoring them. Instead, they are relying on advice from friends and experts to determine what they should buy. Influencers are people that can impact a few people or persuade a large number of people to look at what you have to offer. You need to find influencers for your product, service or idea and then empower them to become evangelists for your cause. These may be affiliates, joint venture partners, bloggers or the media.

In this section of the book, Greg Jameson describes various types of influencers: macro-influencers such as celebrities, and micro-influencers including experts, and family/friends. Each can provide valuable exposure to your business, depending upon your specific goals and objectives.

Remember, influencers are just like you and me. They're regular, everyday folk who have committed to their craft and now have a following. They need content that adds significant value for their tribe. Connect with them and leverage their following to promote your products and services. And that, as Greg explains, is how you can massively increase sales and profits for your business.

Steve Olsher

(@steveolsher) is the New York Times bestselling author of What Is Your WHAT? Discover The ONE Amazing Thing You Were Born To Do, host of the #1 rated radio show/podcast, Reinvention Radio, and creator of the New Media Summit

Chapter 5 – Endorsements & Product Reviews

"People influence people. Nothing influences people more than a recommendation from a trusted friend. A trusted referral influences people more than the best broadcast message. A trusted referral is the Holy Grail of advertising."

- Mark Zuckerberg
Founder and CEO of Facebook

Studies have shown that over 67 percent of all purchase decisions, both online and offline, are influenced by online reviews. Clearly, influencers play a huge impact on what decisions people make. But what (and who) exactly is an influencer? Basically, an influencer is an evangelist for your cause - a brand advocate and niche promoter.

My first experience with influencers happened long before the "influencer effect" was a thing. When I had my software company, Landcadd, we called them "Road Warriors." When you decide to either become an influencer or hire an influencer, understand that you are creating a personal relationship – I remain friends with many of the Landcadd Road Warriors decades later, even though I no longer sell that software.

The Landcadd Road Warriors were hand selected. They were either CAD experts that we trained in the basics of landscape architectural design, or landscape architects that we trained in Computer Aided Design. In both cases, they became experts in our Landcadd software and represented our company in the field when we couldn't be there. They were given a copy of our software to use and we gave them leads for customers who needed training. Then we turned them loose, and they would go out and promote our product with the zeal of an evangelist. This included going to trade shows, conducting seminars, training customers, and even writing articles that would get published in magazines. We even had one person write an entire book about our software!

Today, influencers can reach even larger audiences due to social media. All social influencers have these three basic characteristics in common, to varying degrees:

- Reach: Ability to deliver content to a target audience
- Relevance: Strength of connection to a brand or topic
- Resonance: Ability to drive a desired behavior from an audience

An influencer needs to have a network of people to reach, an authentic connection to a brand or topic, and most importantly—the ability to drive a desired behavior from that network. Every influencer addresses at least one of these core principles:

- Scarcity – the desire to have things that are rare
- Reciprocity – give back to somebody that has given
- Consistency – the desire to be consistent with what we have already said or done

- Authority – Desire to follow the expert
- Similarity – Tendency to be like or follow similar interests of others

There are three basic type of influencers:

- Celebrities: Actors, artists, athletes and media stars who have 1M+ followers and drive 2—5% engagement per post. They have the highest reach on the influencer spectrum, with their influence driven by their celebrity (they tend to be brands in their own right). They have the lowest overall connection when it comes to driving actions on behalf of a brand. After all, who really cares if Justin Bieber tweets about 1-800 flowers?

- Experts: Bloggers, subject-matter practitioners, educators, consultants, authors and speakers who have 10,000 or more followers and drive 5%—25% engagement per post. They have the highest topical relevance on the spectrum, with category-specific influence – such as lifestyle, fashion or business. Of course, the sweet spot is when the expert is also a celebrity, such as Michael Phelps promoting Speedo swim gear, Tiger Woods promoting golf clubs, or Keith Urban promoting guitars. But non-celebrity experts can have a huge impact on your sales and you will want to work with them.

- Family and Friends: These are everyday consumers or employees who have at least 500 followers and drive 25%—50% engagement per post. This means people liking, commenting on, and sharing your posts. These people have the most influence when they are an enthusiast or aficionado of what they are promoting. They have the highest brand relevance and resonance on the spectrum of influencers, with influence driven by their personal experience with a brand and their strength of relationship with their networks. Many multi-level marketing and even insurance and financial companies rely on these micro-influencers to build their brands.

These last two groups are both referred to as micro-influencers. Micro-influencers are social media users unlike typical celebrities or public figures. They're individuals who work or specialize in a particular vertical market and frequently share social media content about their interests. Unlike traditional "macro-influencers," micro-influencers have a more modest number of followers -but they boast hyper-engaged audiences.

The influence of the micro-crowd feels almost counterintuitive, but according to Markerly, an online solution to connect brands with influencers, the like and comment ratio for influencers' Instagram posts actually decreases as their following grows. For influencers with fewer followers, a large percentage will be people they actually know and are thus more likely to trust their recommendations. Micro-influencers are also seen as more authentic because they are less prone to plugging products on a regular basis.

Some of the benefits provided by micro-influencers over macro-influencers:

- Micro-influencers often have a more personal connection with their followers.

  They are real people with a deep passion or subject-matter expertise. They are often more relatable than big-time influencers. Their content can feel more authentic and personal.

- They often have higher engagement rates.

  Micro-influencers' content often performs better than macro-influencers' posts.

- Their audiences are more targeted.

  Many of the social media juggernauts have diverse fan bases. This can be a great thing, but for brands trying to target a particular type of customer, it's better to think narrow. Micro-influencers often cater to a specific, niche audience.

- They are easier to connect with.

  As demand increases, the big names get harder to pin down. People with smaller audiences may be easier to get hold of than superstars.

- They are more affordable.

  A smaller audience can mean a smaller price tag. Of course, brands will need to partner with a number of micro-influencers to achieve scale, but even so, the total cost will often still be lower than the fee commanded by a macro-influencer. And since micro-talent tends to drive higher engagement rates, the overall return on investment or ROI will probably be higher than it would be with a macro-approach.

- Micro-influencers are more authentic.

    Micro-influencers are real people. Their Instagram content is real, too. Instagram users with a few thousand followers likely post their own content, reply to comments, and behave more authentically than a brand or a celebrity with a social media manager might.

All of this is precisely the reason that many companies are willing to provide free products for you to review, even if you are not a celebrity. You have an impact on your following.

Of course, influencer-marketing is not without its challenges, and when you bring more influencers into the picture, those challenges are compounded. It's a lot of work to work with several micro-influencers. Brands have to reach out to them and manage several different relationships. You not only have to manage more personalities but, more importantly, more content. One of the best things to do here is to accept that the content that comes out of each influencer isn't going to be the same. That's okay! If you try to micromanage your micro-influencers, you'll lose what makes them so great in the first place: authenticity. Influencer marketing is a balancing act between reach and relevance, and a micro-approach can be the key to driving massive results.

Whether you want to be a good influencer, or you are looking to engage good influencers, we have to look no further than Dale Carnegie's classic work, "How to Win Friend and Influence People," first published in 1936 (yes influencer marketing has been around long before that). In this book, Carnegie discusses six basic characteristics that you should strive for:

1. Be genuinely interested in the other person.
2. Use their name.
3. Be a good listener.
4. Talk to people about their own interests.
5. Make people feel important and do it sincerely.
6. Smile – Be happy and show it.

The point is, a good influencer isn't trying to sell something. They are trying to be helpful. If you can help readers/listeners/viewers with a solution to their problem, you will be a better influencer. That is why family and friends are often better influencers than celebrities. It is also why, if you want to be known as an expert, that you must show genuine interest in your followers, and not just think of them as a number.

Borrowing Influence

Most of us question our own influence and look to others to help validate who we are – its human nature. Even people who already have a lot of influence feel this way. As a result, you can leverage your own impact by borrowing the influence of others. What I mean is, you can solicit people who are already stars in their own field and raise your own level of influence.

Almost all experts will tell you that they don't have time to sit down with you over a cup of coffee and let you pick their brains for an hour. They want you to pay for their time. You can't simply ask someone for their help because hardly anyone will give it to you, even when they claim that they really want to help others. But what you can do is to cater to their ego by asking them to be a guest on your "Show." Whether you produce a podcast or a video cast, you can usually get anyone to commit to being your special guest when you have a recorded show.

This method works incredibly well. Of course, you actually should have a recorded show. And you should start out by recording yourself for a few episodes, then work your way up to interviewing bigger and bigger experts in your field. That way you will gain experience interviewing and you will have some prior episodes to use as examples.

The great thing is that once you start doing this, you can get people to sit down with you and share their content with you. You can ask them about their business and what works. Ask how your listeners can apply this to their business (and how you can apply it to yours). People who would otherwise never give you the time of day will do this for you because you are doing something for them – namely, giving them an outlet to reach more people and let them talk about themselves.

How often should you do a podcast or video cast? I recommend a minimum of once per month and no more than once per week. Whatever you decide to do, keep it consistent. While live shows, using something like BeLive.tv are great, they are not necessary. You can simply record your interview using Zoom.us and then post it later. You don't even have to have anyone listening, as long as you post it somewhere later that your guest can see it. I recommend that you send your guest a copy of the files and also allow them to use the recording in any way that they see fit. If you are doing a podcast, post it to iTunes for maximum exposure. If you are doing a video cast, post it too YouTube.

Imagine that you are interviewing a superstar in your industry. Now I don't know that you will be able to nail down the biggest players, but you can still get some heavy hitters. For example, I tried to interview Jeff Bezos, the founder and CEO of Amazon, and was never able to make it past his gatekeepers. But when you do interview someone of importance, their status rubs off on you, and your own influence grows as a result. This not only makes it possible to grow your own following, but it makes it easier to work with other influential people and companies going forward.

Review Products

Now you need to select the products you are going to review (or, if you are representing the company, what products you are going to offer to influencers for their review). These products should match your target market. For example, for my scouting-related website, I review products that scouts might use. I always used to get my products for free using one of the following sites:

- Tomoson.com
- Vipon.com (formerly Amazon Review Trader)
- IZEA.com
- SnagShout.com
- amzrc.com (Amazon Review Club)

In October of 2016, Amazon changed their terms of service and no longer allowed companies to offer their products for free in exchange for reviews on Amazon. As such, these sites all had to change the way they did business. Savvy companies took a new approach: they would ask reviewer to buy their products at full price, then leave a review on Amazon. By doing so, you become a "verified purchaser" and are not violating Amazon's terms. Once the review was posted, the company would reimburse you for the cost of the product. Some would provide additional payment as well. If you do this, I suggest working with companies that use a third-party escrow account to ensure that you receive your reimbursement funds.

When Amazon changed their terms of service, the free products I was receiving dried up overnight. Previously, I would get as many as three or four "free" review products per day. Now I was getting approved for only about one product per month, and those products were often not of the same value as before: instead of tents, hammocks, and trekking poles, I might get approved to review a water bottle. This was yet another lesson in not putting all your eggs in one basket — especially a basket that you don't own. You must have multiple income streams and you must own your customers, products, and revenue streams. Whether it be social media, affiliate programs, drop shippers or suppliers, if you don't own it yourself, you are merely renting and you could find your business model destroyed instantly when someone else makes a change.

Of course, there is an advantage to not reviewing too many products. It has been said that scarcity is as big a motivator as a "recommendation" is. That is why Amazon tells you "Order soon – only 5 left in stock". By posting reviews less frequently, they become rarer, which leads to them being more effective.

Because the review sites are no longer the best way to get free products, I suggest contacting the companies you want to associate yourself with directly. The review sites I mentioned previously are still an effective way of contacting companies looking for reviews, but you need to establish your own relationship with them. People now seek me out asking me to review their products. I don't pay for the privilege of reviewing a product – companies either send me product for free or even pay me to review their products. I concentrate on scouting related items (for Cyberbase Trading Post), or technology-related items (for WebStores Ltd). When leaving a review, don't just write a few sentences – spend some time and write a review that the company will notice so they will see the benefit in having you review their products. Create YouTube videos about the products, and make them of high enough quality that the company will want to use them and promote them as well (which helps to promote you).

For example, I recently reviewed a waterproof dry sack. This was an ideal product for Cyberbase, as scouts enjoy many water sports including white-water rafting, canoeing, rowing, sailing, and even camping in wet conditions. For my product review, I made a video of me placing a roll of toilet paper inside the dry bag. Then I put in a 25-pound anvil as well to weigh it down. I put the dry bag into my hot tub and shook it up and down multiple times. After I was sure that the contents were well soaked, I retrieved the content and the roll of toilet paper was still bone-dry. I used the video in my blog, on YouTube, and posted it on my social media pages.

Not only did my readers appreciate this thorough review (I know this because many of them bought it through my affiliate link), the company also found it useful enough that they asked me to review other products they had to offer. What was even better for the company was that my video was linked to my blog post, and this allowed that article to get listed on page one of Google, right after the Amazon listing. That is the reason why companies will hire (and re-hire) you to write reviews. It is great social proof when you can provide them quality content.

For another review, I was asked to review a Kold water bottle. This was a water bottle that is double insulated and is supposed to keep water cold for up to 8 hours. Now, I go on lots of bike rides, and this is in fact a problem. The water gets warm before you have a chance to drink it, even when you put ice in the water. So, during the review, I decided to set the Kold water bottle next to a regular insulated water bottle and place them both in the sun. I took the temperature of the water in both bottle at the beginning. Then I let them sit in the sun for two hours. Then I took the water temperature again. The water in the regular water bottle had gone up to 115 degrees! The water in the Kold bottle had barely risen. This showed how well the bottle worked and of course it got a 5-star review. Again, if you are going to write product reviews, make the review worth the time for someone to read it. Both your readers and the company will get more value from it, and you will sell more with your affiliate links.

FTC regulations

Endorsements are an important tool for advertisers and they can be persuasive to consumers. But the law says they also have to be truthful and not misleading. The FTC's Guides Concerning the Use of Endorsements and Testimonials in Advertising are guidelines designed to help advertisers of all types including – TV, print, radio, blogs, word-of-mouth marketing – make sure that they meet this standard. You can find these guidelines at:

http://bit.ly/ftcregs

In August of 2016, the United States government noticed a large upswing in celebrity endorsements and began to crack down. While Amazon claims that the reason for changing their "terms and conditions" was because of public pressure about paid reviews, I suspect it had more to do with the government applying pressure to the company. Or, perhaps they just wanted to control the reviews more themselves, as they still offer their paid Vine program. Either way, paid reviews on Amazon are no longer noticeable.

After reading the guidelines above, you might be inclined to forget about influencer marketing. I encourage you to not do that. Recommendations and endorsements by others is how Amazon built its business and how you can grow yours as well. Just be sure that you (or your influencers) put a disclaimer on every email, blog post, YouTube video, etc. that involves a monetary exchange. Here is an example:

Disclaimer: *I received this product at either a discount or for free for my honest, fair, and unbiased opinion. All opinions in my reviews are my own and are not swayed in any way due to receiving a discount. I am under no obligation to write a review, the choice was purely my own and I received no compensation.*

If you are promoting products via an email or your blog and you are receiving an affiliate commission for it, the FTC says you must disclose this as well. Just do it, and let people know that you wouldn't promote something that you didn't believe in.

Negative Reviews

While Amazon and the FTC are concerned about fake positive reviews, a bigger concern for many businesses is fake negative reviews. I was reading an article in USA Today about a Massachusetts man having to pay more than $30K for writing a negative Yelp review. Apparently, he was an employee of a jewelry store trash-talking a competing jewelry store. These kinds of negative reviews are more common than you might think and they are incredibly hard to remove once they've been posted.

I spend some time later in this book discussing Facebook advertising, which if your company does not have a stellar reputation, can actually backfire on you. For example, I recently saw an ad for an airline that was new to the Denver market and was offering $199 tickets to London. The responses to the ad in the comments field were scathing – having the exact opposite effect that the airline was trying to accomplish.

What this means, of course, is that you must have a great reputation in the marketplace. My friend Peter Brissette, who specializes in reputation management and review marketing, likes to tell people that the best way to get rid of a negative review is to not get one in the first place. This isn't just a trite comment, you should establish your online reputation in such a way that if anyone ever was too post something negative about you, that no one would believe it.

Reviews and testimonials may have the biggest impact on your business than anything else you can do. That is why influencer marketing is so important.

The Role of Sponsors

Sponsors can play a big part in your success – whether you are the sponsoring organization or the one who is being sponsored. It's like endorsing each other. Remember, this is a two-way street. A sponsor is not going to simply give you money. They need something in exchange. Speedo pays Michael Phelps a lot of money, but in exchange, Michael Phelps endorses their products and promotes them. If you are going to find sponsors, you must do the same. If you are the one who is going to sponsor an organization, you will want to find one that closely aligns with your business and can help promote you.

My first experience with being sponsored was with Dell Computers. At the time, Michael Dell had just moved out of his dorm room and I had purchased one of his earlier machines called PC's Limited. In 1987, he changed the name of his company to be Dell Computer Corporation, but very few people had heard of that name. I met a fellow named Randy Andes, who worked for Dell, at a trade show. At the time, my company, Landcadd, Inc. was selling some software I had written that sat on top of AutoCAD. Dell wanted to break into the computer reseller market and not just rely on their own direct sales. And Landcadd had over 100 dealers at the time who were selling our software. As part of becoming a Landcadd dealer, you were required to attend a training class that we gave so you could learn our software. The problem was that we needed machines to fill our computer lab. And Dell needed access to our dealers. This was a perfect win-win situation, and Dell supplied us with twelve computers to outfit our training lab. It didn't cost us anything. The dealers got exposed to Dell computers, many of whom ended up selling them.

This worked so well that we decided to see who else might give us free stuff. When we went to trade shows, most of the other companies had big fancy booths that costs tens of thousands of dollars. Here is what we came up with: since we sold landscape software, what if we could make our booth be a park gazebo? This would not only make us stand out from all the high-tech booths at a software show, but it would tie into what we were selling. We struck a deal with WH Porter, a manufacturer of park gazebos. The credit for this really goes to my wife, Jill. She called up Bill Porter and explained to him what we wanted to do. We would put their park structures into our software as 3D symbols that landscape architects could simply drop into their CAD drawings. These symbols would contain attributes that identified them as a specific Porter design. In exchange, they would deliver and setup one of their gazebos at our various trade shows for the next year. And by the way, could they paint it green and black to match our corporate colors? They did! This again worked well for both parties, and that is the essence of a sponsorship.

Think of a sponsorship as an influencer on steroids. Both parties must benefit.

I know a photographer who teaches classes on photography. He is sponsored by several camera companies including Canon. He is also sponsored by his tripod manufacturer and various other camera gadgets. This is a great concept – he gets all the latest camera gear in exchange for him promoting their products at his seminars.

The reason why this works, of course, goes back to what this chapter is all about, empowering influencers. It's simple - influencers help sell products. If you want to sell more products, you need to work with those in your market who can reach your final consumer.

The Magic T-Shirt

When we were selling our Landcadd software, we sold through a dealer and distribution channel rather than selling direct. It cost $3,000 to become a dealer, which included two copies of the software (one for demonstration purposes and one to re-sell). This was in the mid-1980's and three-grand was a sizable investment. Often when we were talking to a potential dealer, they would almost back out of the deal. We'd tell them how we were doing national advertising and were going to give them leads every month, but that wouldn't work to convince them. We'd tell them we were going to train them on the software and provide support to them, but that wasn't a deciding factor. We'd tell them how they got a 40% margin on everything they sold, but that still didn't close the sale. Then we'd ask them what size of t-shirt they wore. "Why?", they wanted to know. "Because we are going to include a free t-shirt as part of your dealer package." That would always close the sale!

Landcadd had some really cool t-shirts. One of the more popular ones had our logo on the front breast, with a saying that read "Make your Vision a '*Virtual*' Reality." On the back of the shirt was a super-hero looking guy wearing virtual reality glasses and a motion-sensor glove with text that read "Landcadd Cyberpunk Workforce – Welcome to the Future!" Remember, this was the mid 1980's, and we were experimenting with VR using the 3D CAD models that our software would generate. At one trade show, we brought in some VR equipment and let the landscape architects immerse themselves into their designs, picking up trees and other objects and moving them around in real-time in 3D. It's not that big of a deal now, but back then we had people lined up for up to an hour and half waiting at our booth to try this out.

We also used these t-shirts as bribes for the union employees when we were setting up for a trade show. Working with unions to set up a booth like the gazebo I mentioned before was challenging to say the least. But it was amazing what the workers would do when you promised them one of our t-shirts. We'd always get special treatment using the t-shirts as collateral. Since our software worked on top of AutoCAD, we'd also provide our t-shirts to select Autodesk employees as well, who we thought would promote our products. It worked wonders.

Years later, as my children rode the school bus, they noticed that the bus driver was wearing a Landcadd t-shirt! They told him, "hey, that's my dad's company!" He didn't believe it at first (and neither could I believe that one of my "magic t-shirts" ended up on a school bus driver). But the power of t-shirts is enormous.

And it's not just the young crowd. Professional business men wear t-shirt as well, albeit when they are relaxing and having fun with their friends rather than at a business meeting. But that is exactly the time and the people you want to reach with your message. A person's close friends can have a conversation about your brand. Sure, you could make a polo shirt or a tie to give-away to corporate types, but the reason why t-shirts are magical is that they break down barriers.

I still own all my Landcadd t-shirts, and in fact am wearing one as I write this. I was listening to a podcast recently and the narrator was talking about using free t-shirts to promote his products, like he had thought of this and that it was the best marketing idea to hit the planet. Sorry, this idea has been around long before I started using them in the 1980's. But I thought about what makes t-shirts so magical. Why do people climb over each other at ball games to get a free t-shirt being thrown into the crowd by the cheerleaders? Why do people buy so many t-shirts when they go on vacation and visit a certain place?

The answer is that we all want to belong. Employers who create logo merchandise for their employees tend to have more loyal employees, because they feel like they belong to the group. And guess what? Customers like to feel like they are part of something special as well. T-shirts help to provide that sense of being part of something.

Now, I don't recommend getting a plain white t-shirt with nothing but your logo on it. You need to get a quality t-shirt and have something creative on it. T-shirts are incredible conversation starters when done right. Think about a sky-diving business. Including a t-shirt as part of the adventure would insure that anyone that went skydiving with them would proudly wear it in front of all their friends. Not only would this be a great conversation starter, it would almost insure that any of their adventurous friends would want to go skydiving as well.

When my kids were little, the local orthodontist sponsored every sports team in our town. His logo and tag line were on the back of every sports jersey there was. And guess who the parents took their kids to when they needed braces? These kids and their parents became walking billboards for this orthodontist. But more importantly, they became advocates.

As a business owner, imagine if all of your customers were to become your salesforce, simply because you gave them one of your magic t-shirts. This is one of the best marketing investments you can make. Sure, you can (and probably should), create more expensive logo merchandise, but the t-shirt idea works best whenever you include it as part of your package to your re-sellers, customers, and other influencers.

My friend, Joel Comm, recently created a t-shirt that says "Do Good Stuff", with the OO in Good being a sort of smiley face character in sunglasses. He also created stickers with the same graphics, and he signs his books this way. The message is strong, and so are the graphics, so the shirt has become a great marketing piece for him. And it also serves as a conversation starter. You want people to do this for your brand. Not only do people wear the shirt, but they post pictures of themselves wearing it. In fact, you could easily create a contest asking people to show themselves doing fun (or funny) things while wearing your shirt.

Social media and the selfie make it possible for even more people to be reached when people want to be part of your tribe. You want them wearing your message and being a walking billboard. When they feel like they are a part of what you are doing, they will want to promote your message and they will become loyal customers and advocates, helping to spread the word.

Once people are emotionally attached to your brand, they may even want to sell your products and services for you. I'll talk more about his in the next chapter – "Engage Affiliates."

Chapter 6 – Engage Affiliates

"I'd rather have 1% of the effort of 100 men than 100% of my own effort."

- J. Paul Getty
Founder of Getty Oil

Once a consumer decides they are in need of a product or service, they start with a short list of options based on initial brand awareness. TV, radio, print, word-of-mouth, online display advertising, social media and affiliates all play an ongoing role in shaping a consumer's awareness of their brand options. But when a consumer sees that a product has been tested, evaluated, and recommended by someone, they take that recommendation seriously. That is what an affiliate program can do for you.

I believe that every business should have an affiliate program. Here's why: Think of affiliates as being like Oprah. Whenever Oprah would recommend a product, the sales of that product go up. That is what affiliate sales can do for your business.

If we look again at Amazon as the example to follow, we see that Amazon derives about 40% of its sales from affiliates. Everyone already knows about Amazon, yet they still derive a huge portion of their sales from other people driving customers to their websites. Amazon Associates (affiliates) receive a commission for referring customers to Amazon by placing links on their websites to Amazon, if the referral results in a sale.

The mistake that most people make is to simply use the canned ads provided by the company offering the affiliate program. This is the least effective way to earn an affiliate commission. Like everything else, you need to make it personal for your buyer persona. As my friend, Ken McArthur says, *"The key to success with affiliate sales is that you have to invest into promoting a product as though it were your own."*

If you are looking to create an affiliate program for your business, consider hand-picking affiliates and making them a super-affiliate or joint venture (JV) partner. These are people who will help to sell your products as if they were the one who created it, not just inserting an ad.

I am an Amazon Associate (the name of their affiliate program). Whenever I review a product for someone, I can determine if I like the product well enough to recommend it. And If I can recommend it, I want to make money.

Let's say that I have reviewed a set of carbon fiber trekking poles and wrote a blog about it on my Cyberbase Trading Post site. Yes, I got a free set of trekking poles, but as an affiliate, I would like to recommend this product and get a commission for anyone who buys the poles as a result of my reviews. I don't just use the canned ads that Amazon provides, but I am proactive with my Amazon affiliate links. Each blog post contains a minimum of three links to the product: two text links and one link on the product photo. I always shorten the links using Amazon's tool so they don't look intimidating. For example, you can get the trekking poles I'm referring to at:

http://amzn.to/2IPubxA.

I also create YouTube videos about those products. In the description of the video I place the shortened affiliate link as well. I create social network posts that also include affiliate links to the product. For example, I might create an Instagram post about the product. Instagram is interesting because it works well for influencers. But it was designed to share photos from your cell phone. As a marketer, you often want to modify your images, add text to them, or create infographics. You might even want to add your shortened affiliate link as text to an image. Instagram wasn't designed for that, but you can get around this shortcoming by using an Android emulation program on your laptop called BlueStacks.

The point is, affiliate links should be included in all your social media posts. This is how you get paid. Your readers are relying on your recommendations, so I use the affiliate links liberally.

Another thing you might want to consider trying is building Amazon affiliate links to lists that you create. You can create as many lists of products as you want and group like items together, then share those lists with others. Amazon does not provide a default affiliate link to your lists, but you can create one by using the "any page affiliate link." Go to your affiliate page and select product Linking > Link to Any Page. Choose the far-right tab that is titled, "Link to Any Page," and enter in the URL string when you are viewing a particular list. For example,

I created a list of all the products I use in my "Biking with Greg" videos. I created a link to this page, which gives you a long HTML string. Then, you can copy the URL out of the code provided, and shorten it with bit.ly. You can see the result at

http://bit.ly/bikingwithgreg

The standard Amazon affiliate link gives you 24 hours for a customer to make a purchase in order for you to earn a commission.

If you can get people to visit the Amazon site (pretty much for any reason) a percentage of them will naturally end up buying something. The cool thing is that whether or not they buy the thing you linked to, **you still earn a commission**!

This means that if a customer clicks your link and orders anything, within a 24-hour window, you'll earn a commission on those items. It's a universal cookie, meaning that even if the customer clicks through your link to view a set of trekking poles, but ends up buying a new tent or sleeping bag (or even something unrelated like new speakers for their computer), you'll get paid for all of those items.

Based on my experience, only about 25% of my affiliate commissions come from products I specifically linked the customer to. So, without the universal cookie, my commissions would be a lot lower. As soon as the customer places an order, your cookie is wiped away. Even if they come back 1 hour later and order more things, you won't get paid.

Sometimes though, a customer doesn't immediately order a product, especially if it's a high-ticket item. To make up for this, Amazon will extend your cookie by another 89 days if the customer adds a product (any product) to their cart after following your affiliate link. In other words, if they add it to the cart and then leave Amazon, you've got 89 more days to hope they come back and finish checking out.

So, what if you could make a link that would automatically add your recommendation to their Amazon cart? You can! Use the following code to make an add to cart link of your own:

Replace "webstores01-20" with your Associates ID and "B01I8S42YK" with the ASIN of the Amazon product you wish to promote. If you are a Product Advertising API subscriber, you should also replace the Subscription ID as follows:

```
<form method="GET"
action="http://www.amazon.com/gp/aws/cart/add.html">
<input type="hidden" name="AssociateTag" value="webstores01-
20?/>
 <input type="hidden" name="SubscriptionId"
value="[AWSAccessKeyId]"/>
<input type="hidden" name="ASIN.1? value=" B01I8S42YK?/>
<br/>
 <input type="hidden" name="Quantity.1? value="1?/>
<br/>
<input type="image" name="add" value="Buy from Amazon.com"
border="0? alt="Buy from Amazon.com"
src="http://images.amazon.com/images/G/01/associates/add-to-
cart.gif">
 </form>
```

However, this DOESN'T mean that if the customer adds a product to their cart, you now have a 90-day cookie and can earn on anything else they buy in the next 90 days. You only get a commission if they buy that specific item, so it is a trade-off. If you send a customer to the "add to cart" page, and all they see is a blank page with the question, "do you want to add this to your cart?" with the name of the product, they may simply close the tab. If you use the standard affiliate link that shows them the product information, reviews, related products and pricing, it might be more likely to result in a sale. Creating a link to send them directly to the shopping cart might have the opposite effect, so be careful.

I have found that the best way to generate affiliate commissions is to simply help someone decide what to buy. Don't try to sell them something. This is why review links work so much better than the fixed ads.

Here is a good example of this from one of my clients:

My customer had produced a line of nutrition bars, similar to many of the "Power Bars" that are on the market today. Since there was a lot of competition as more and more bars were coming out, he needed a way to get this product seen. Traffic to his website was slow, and he was only making a few sales a week. I suggested that he try affiliate marketing. He needed to find a power blogger in the health food industry.

Luckily for him, he was able to meet Isabel De Los Rios, the founder and creator of Beyond Diet. Isabel was a working mom, a certified nutritionist, a best-selling author, and most importantly she had helped over half a million people. She had a big list. And my customer was able to sign her up as an affiliate. We created an affiliate code for Beyond Diet using the Affiliate Royale software. Beyond Diet then did two things. It gave an email blast to their list and a blog post. The success was so overwhelming, that the first time they did this, it brought down our servers. We had to have them do it again after we upgraded the plan. Within a week, my customer had to rent a commercial kitchen in order to handle all the orders. Here is what that blog post looked like:

Energy Bars are Not Your Best Option...Eat This Instead

Why shouldn't you be buying those "healthy" energy bars you see on the store shelves? Just take a look at the ingredients on the label. Many of them contain cheap protein, soy, high fructose corn syrup) or concentrated fruit juices, which are high in fructose) and piles of synthetic vitamins. But we have found an energy bar out there which lives up to its name and includes only natural and organic ingredients. Just Energy Nutrients bars (JEN bars) will truly nourish your body.

At this point in the blog, there is a picture of Isabel holding up the JEN bars, with a caption that says,

"JEN bars are the first bars I have found that are not only delicious, but contain completely 'Isabell-approved' raw, organic ingredients... perfect for any healthy fat loss plan."

The article continues...

What exactly is a JEN bar?

JEN bar (Just Energy Nutrients) is a unique energy bar unlike any other on the market. The JEN bar is made with a unique blend of natural and organic ingredients designed to sustain a body's energy for several hours.

At this point, there is a break in her blog post with a graphic that reads,

"Don't just take Isabel's word, order your JEN bars today!"

Of course, when you click on this graphic, there is an affiliate link to the JEN bars site where you can place your order. The article continues…

Why do I love JEN bars?

Because JEN bars only contain raw nuts, as roasting causes fats and oils to go rancid, increasing free-radical damage to your body. They also contain ingredients such as butter and walnuts to boost the body's omega-3 and omega-6 fatty acids. The combination of sesame and flax seed meal helps reduce the body's high blood serum cholesterol value. And buckwheat is a source of natural fiber, magnesium, and vitamin B. These bars are also Gluten Free.

How do they taste?

Absolutely amazing! I love these bars as a mid-morning snack or afternoon treat. They are so incredibly filling and will help curb any afternoon cravings.

Ingredients

The makers of JEN bars only use the most natural, high quality, organic raw ingredients.

Almonds, Walnuts, Coconut, Sunflower Seeds, Flax Seed Meal, Sesame Seeds, Buckwheat, Dark Chocolate, Carob, Peanut Butter, Butter

At this point, there is another graphic which reads, **"Try a JEN Bar >>> >>> >>> Order Yours Now!"**, which of course, contains her affiliate link to order the product.

Can you see how much more effective this is than just using one of the pre-built ads? When your affiliates step up to the plate like this, it can absolutely sky-rocket your sales overnight. And if you are the affiliate trying to earn commissions, this type of approach will out-perform the standard banner ads many times over, especially if you have built a readership that trusts your opinions.

As an affiliate, here are the things you can do so that you can become a power blogger:

- Build traffic to your Blog
- Build loyalty and trust with your readers
- Think about the intent of your readers
- Find relevant products to promote
- Use Social Proof.
- Use reviews
- Share informational links
- Link images.
- Share multiple affiliate links per post
- Make genuine recommendations
- Use "Buy Now" Buttons

> *Social Proof, also known as informational social influence, is a psychological phenomenon where people assume the actions of others in an attempt to reflect correct behavior for a given situation.*

Setting up your own affiliate program

Affiliates can make some money by selling your products, but most affiliates do this as a way to earn some additional income, not to make a living at it. The real winners in the affiliate game are the companies that run the affiliate programs: Amazon, Target, Walmart, and YOU!

Yes, you can run an affiliate program and get others to market and sell on your behalf. If you run an ecommerce website, I recommend that you do this. Why not get another 40% increase in your sales by creating a team of virtual salespeople? There are two primary ways to do this: 1) use a third-party affiliate program like Commission Junction or Link Share, or 2) manage your own program using a plugin or app like Affiliate Royale or iDevAffiliate.

Third Party Affiliate Management Programs

There are some very good reasons to use third-party management companies. For starters, many affiliates will go to these sites looking for product to promote. You get a lot of exposure that you wouldn't get otherwise and are more likely to sign up affiliates this way. You don't have to track anything. These sites do that for you. You simply put up your ads and list your products – it is still a lot of work, but these sites do all the heavy lifting for you.

If you are selling physical products, both Commission Junction and Link Share are good choices. Walmart uses Link Share, so you know they are capable of running a good affiliate program. If you are selling downloadable digital products like software, eBooks, music, 3D printer files, etc. then a good choice is JV Zoo.

All of these sites make money by requiring that you pay them – either an upfront listing fee and/or a percentage of the sale. Because of this, you may have to qualify by proving to them that you make a certain number of sales each month.

As I said, you will have to create banner ads to upload onto these sites, so that your affiliates can then use these ads on their blogs. Best practice is to change out your banner ads monthly, or at least quarterly, to give your affiliates a season-specific ad to run. You should also upload individual products with affiliate links directly to those products so that your affiliates can recommend and link to specific products. As I showed earlier, this is the best way to generate sales.

Direct Management of Affiliates

Perhaps you would prefer to manage your affiliate program yourself rather than paying for a third-party service. This of course is what Amazon does. Amazon runs their own affiliate program. But direct management of affiliate programs isn't just for big companies like Amazon. In fact, this may be a better choice for small companies. By using a plugin like Affiliate Royale or iDevAffiliate, you can run your own affiliate program right on your website.

The big advantage to this approach is that you control everything. You don't have to pay a third party (although you may have to purchase the plugin). You don't have to be approved. You just start doing it. You can more easily hand-pick who you want to be promoting your products. A big disadvantage, of course, is that your affiliate program won't have the added exposure that a third-party management site would provide.

You will still have to create banner ads and product links for your affiliates to use. You will also be responsible for paying the affiliates yourself. These plugins will track all this for you, but you must be actively involved.

An affiliate program requires effort on your part as a store owner to make it effective. It also requires work on the part of your affiliates to be promoting your products. You will want to give them all the tools that you can to make them successful, as it can greatly impact your sales. Keep your affiliates informed about what is going on with your business. Keep them happy and pay them well, typically 50% of your profits. For a physical item, if you make a 20% profit, you would split that with your affiliate and give them a 10% commission. For a digital product that is 100% profit, they might earn 50%. If this seems like a lot, consider what it would cost you to have an in-house salesperson. Then consider how much a good affiliate could add to your bottom line. You'll soon see why Amazon continues to use this marketing technique and why you should as well.

That is not to say that Amazon does everything correctly with their affiliate program. They have a low commission structure, typically 4 to 8 percent. It takes two months to get paid. You can do better.

Here's the thing: if you are going to run an affiliate program for your business (which I recommend you do), treat your affiliates like commissioned employees (they are). Pay them well, and pay them in a timely manner, so that they remain excited about promoting your products for you.

Chapter 7 – Earn Even More

"The aim of marketing is to know and understand the customer so well the product or service fits him and sells itself."

- Peter Drucker
Management Consultant

Sadly, during all my years of building ecommerce websites and consulting with store owners, I have too often seen websites that have no life to them. The pictures are either generic images that every site selling that product uses, or they are of poor quality showing the item sitting on a shelf in their store. The product titles are generic as well. Often the descriptions about the product are either non-existent or only a sentence or two. In short, there is absolutely nothing that would make a person want to buy that product from you. The solution is not that difficult, but you must put some effort into it.

Remember at the beginning of this book when we talked about giving away a free product in exchange for getting the customer's email? We had to think like the customer. What could we offer that was valuable enough to make the customer want to share their information with us? Creating product detail pages is similar: if I was a customer, what would I want to know about this product in order for me to make a buying decision? It turns out that more detailed product pages are better. A DemandGen Report backs this up: 95% of buyers chose a solution provider that "Provided them with ample content to help navigate through each stage of the buying process." The more information you provide, the more likely the consumer will have the information they need to get them to purchase from you. Here's how to do it:

1. Create a Buyer Persona
   You should know exactly who your target customer is. Clearly, in the case of Cyberbase Trading Post, this is scout leaders. But certain products might be for young mothers (of cub scout-aged boys), while other products might be for middle-aged men (who have older sons in a high adventure troop). Your product page should speak directly to your buyer persona as if you were having a one-on-one conversation with that specific person.

2. Create Buyer Persona Product Titles
   It is rare that you should use the name of the product as supplied by the manufacturer as your product title. This is too generic. Instead, craft your titles to speak to the person you are selling to. For example, I sell fake candles on Cyberbase (which can be useful for scouting ceremonies). Instead of a title like:

Fake Candles

Do this instead:

The Perfect Artificial Candle that is Ideal for Fire Restrictions or Windy Outdoor Scout Ceremonies

The concept here is that you are appealing to your specific buyer. All of your product titles should do this.

3. Show Your Product in Context

   The generic images of your products as supplied by the manufacturer are used by every site on the internet selling the same product as you. You want your product detail pages to stand out. The best way to do this is to show the product in action. In the case of the fake candles, take a photograph of a scout "lighting" (turning on) the candle during a ceremony. This could be an indoor ceremony in a building that doesn't allow open flames. Take another photo of an outdoor ceremony showing the candles remaining "lit," even though the wind is blowing. Use multiple images to tell your story.

   In addition, not instead of, include a video showing the product being used. Video is way under-utilized on ecommerce web sites. Video is your opportunity to sell your product as if you were the salesperson face-to-face with a customer who walked in your physical brick and mortar store. People like to watch the internet much more than they like to read the internet. So, make a short 1 to 2-minute video about the product. Make sure you show how the product is being used, not just you standing there saying "we also offer these fake candles." If you are selling a cooking gadget, create a video of you using the cooking gadget. Show the product in action!

There is another very good reason to create a product video for every one of your products, and that is search engine placement. Search Engine Optimization or SEO is a question that almost everyone asks about. "How can I get listed on page one of Google?" seems to be the common thing that business owners want to know. This is the answer. You should upload your videos to YouTube. You will end up with an entire "channel" of every item in your store. The video titles should mimic your product titles, targeting your buyer persona. The description of the video on YouTube must contain a link back to the product page where you are selling that item. To create this link, simply enter the entire URL string in the description, including the http:// prefix. Simply saying, "you can buy this at www.mysite.com" is not enough to generate the link. You must say "this product is available for purchase at
http://www.mysite.com/fake-candles"

When you do this, Google (which owns YouTube) will follow that link using their "bots" back to the page on your website that is actually selling the fake candles (or whatever you are demonstrating). When the bot arrives at your product page, it will see that this page is in fact talking about the fake candles and will assume that the page must be really important as it relates to fake candles and will push you to the top of the search results for that search term. So, having a video for each of your products helps to not only engage with your customers, but also helps those customers find you in the first place. Take the time to do this for all your products. It is worth it.

4. Craft Buyer Persona Specific Product Descriptions
   Most websites do not provide enough detail about their products. Don't simply say:

   Fake Candles. Can be used for scout ceremonies.

   Dan & Chip Heath, NYT Best-Selling authors, tell us that after a presentation, 63% of attendees remember stories, while only 5% remember statistics. The same is true with sales copy, so tell a story. Remember, you are the expert on what you are selling. Your customer may know very little about your product. This is what content marketing is all about, providing content. People come to the internet looking for information, so give it to them. Don't hold back because you think you are being too verbose. It is highly unlikely that this is the case. So, don't just use a short terse description like the previous example. Try to engage with your buyer persona with something like this instead:

   Does your scout unit meet in a church, school or other building that prohibits the use of open flames? You want to use candles as part of your scout ceremonies, but you are not allowed to – until now!

Any scout unit can now use candles as part of their ceremonies by using these faux candles because they not only look real but are 100% safe.

These artificial candles look exactly like a real candle. They are made of real wax so they not only look real, they even feel real! The "flames" flicker and dance so you can't tell the difference, even when close-up.

Lighting the candles can be done with the remote control switch, which allows you to make the motion as if you were actually lighting the candle. Instead, you simply push a button to turn on the flame. The flame is created by using an LED light that shines on a piece of moving plastic that is shaped like a flame. This gives it the effect of a real candle flame. These are so realistic that we've even had the fire department called when we were using them. Talk about creating an event that your scouts will not soon forget!

Another common problem with candles at scout ceremonies is that outdoor ceremonies make using candles almost impossible. Even the slightest breeze will usually blow out the candles. These artificial candles remain "lit" even in windy conditions. Their long battery life insures that the candles won't go out half-way through your ceremony. Don't spoil the effect of the ceremony by having your flames extinguished. Be sure to buy twelve of these – one for each point of the Scout Law.

Specifications:
* *SIZE: 8" tall x 3" diameter*
Made of plastic and coated with real wax
* *SAFE – eliminates fire hazards compared with real burning candles, ensuring safety around children, pets and adults*
* *FREE REMOTE – we are currently offering a FREE remote control with every purchase*
* *MOVING WICK – flameless, natural moving wick simulates authentic flame movement*
* *5-HOUR TIMER – environmentally conscious and cost effective 5-hour timer function*
* *BATTERY LIFE: 60- hour battery life (requires 2 D batteries, not included)*
* *CLEAN – no burnt-out wax and wicks and allows a pollution-free, pure air environment. No need to keep re-buying candles*
* *REAL IVORY WAX – looks and feels just like a real candle*
* *100% MONEY BACK GUARANTEE*

Yes, that description appears to be long-winded, but studies have shown that longer copy sells more on the internet than short copy. In fact, the average word count of pages that ranked on the first page of Google for a given search term is a little over 2,000 words. The above copy is less than 400 words, so don't be afraid of saying too much.

This product description follows a tried and tested formula that you should follow:

- The first paragraph talks about the problem or their pain.

- The second paragraph is courtesy Ray Edwards, one of the premier copy-writers in the world who is responsible for generating hundreds of millions in revenues. Ray calls this your unique core thesis. The structure is like this:

  Any [*your audience*] **can** [*describe the solution*] **by using** [*your product or service*] **because** [*how it solves the problem*].

- The next few paragraphs are used to appeal to their emotions and describe the benefits they get by using your products. It is best to use real stories if you can and show how your product solves the problem.

- Conclude the body of the copy with a call to action. In the example above, I suggest that they buy 12 candles – one for each point of the Scout Law. Ray Edwards suggests making the call to action include a "what if" question: *What if you don't purchase these candles? You can continue to not have the ability to use candles at your ceremonies. You can continue to have your ceremonies be forgetful and uninteresting. Or you can choose to purchase these candles and make your scout ceremonies something that the boys will remember for years to come.*

This may or may not be appropriate on all product detail pages, but a call to action is certainly recommended.

- Finally, (and this is sometimes on a separate tab), you list the features and specifications for those that want this detailed information. This is especially useful for technical products like cameras or water pumps. Specifications are best displayed in a table or as bullet points. But this should never be the focus of your copy. You should always concentrate on benefits, not features.

Invest in the time to craft a detailed product description and target that description at the exact person (buyer persona) who you are trying to sell to. This will pay huge dividends.

5. Reinforce with Social Proof
   Yes, this goes back to the previous two chapters. You need to let others share their experiences with your product, both by providing customer reviews and testimonials as well as posts and stories from social media. Just like Amazon, you want one customer to sell

other customers on why they should by this product from you. Customer reviews are huge when it comes to influencing others to buy. People are much more likely to take the word of a total stranger about your products than they are from you (after all, you are the salesman). This is true in spite of the fact that you have established yourself as the expert and have shown that your site is all about helping them. Let your customers do the talking!

Eliminate Excess Products

When you run an ecommerce business, you will end up with excess products. This might be because you purchased too many of something and you have it in inventory, or because you have been doing reviews for products that people have sent to you and you don't really need the product. Here are some creative ways to earn even more money while getting rid of your un-wanted inventory.

If you don't want or need products, you can sell the un-needed items on eBay. This is a great way to generate some extra revenue. What I like to do with products that I have reviewed is give them away as part of a monthly raffle. To qualify for the raffle, you must be part of the premium membership program. I randomly select one of my premium members and give them one of my excess products, and announce this in my newsletter. This is a great way to create loyal followers or even evangelists for your products.

A: Amplify Your Message

"Stopping advertising to save money is like stopping your watch to save time."

- Henry Ford

FOREWORD by Andrea Vahl

People simply don't find you. You must reach out to them. That is what this section of Greg's book is all about, amplifying your message through advertising, automated emails, and attending live events.

Facebook ads are becoming CRITICAL and that's not a bad thing, because they can help you get massive results in your business!

What I've seen from many clients I've worked with is that they have tried a couple of Facebook ads on their own and they say they just don't work. But the reason they didn't work was that they were running them in the wrong way. So, of course, they aren't going to work. You need the right strategies, the right tracking, and the right budget to make sure Facebook ads work well for you.

To make advertising be effective, requires not only a budget, but the right kind of ad to match your goal, good targeting, and split testing. Running ads simultaneously and comparing them to each other is called split testing, and this is crucial for determining what ads are most effective.

The largest part of your advertising budget should be getting email opt-ins. Many businesses feel like social media doesn't work because they don't know what success looks like. They want sales from social media but they aren't measuring inbound leads and tracking them. To do this, you need to have special email lists or tags in your system to show when people are opting in.

Make sure you deliver value through your email newsletter to keep people engaged. Don't just send out marketing messages. If you consistently deliver value, you will' have a better open rate and you will have a better conversion when you do send out an email with a sales message.

You've seen the message through this book about delivering value. That is the key point when it comes to amplifying your message. Deliver value and let your customers spread the word.

Andrea Vahl
Co-Author, Facebook Marketing for Dummies
Facebook Advertising Secrets Course
http://www.andreavahl.com/

Chapter 8 – Advertising

"Never stop testing and your advertising will never stop improving."

- David Ogilvy
The Father of Advertising

In the last section, I spent a considerable amount of time discussing how affiliates do better writing their own copy and making a personal recommendation than they do by using banner ads. Does this mean that you shouldn't advertise? Absolutely not! In fact, with the changes that both Google and Facebook have made over the past few years, it is now imperative that you advertise. Let me explain.

In February of 2016, Google decided they weren't making enough money and therefore wanted more of yours. Depending upon what you are searching for, the company now only displays ads "above the fold," what is visible on the screen before you have to scroll. They then show the first 10 organic listings (which of course keep changing based upon their latest algorithm updates), followed by more ads. To show up on page one of Google for certain search terms now requires that you advertise with them.

Facebook has also gotten greedier. Since 2012, the organic reach of posts made to a business page has steadily declined, from sixteen percent to less than two percent. This means that if you have 1000 likes on your page, and you post something to that page, Facebook will show that post to fewer than twenty of your fans. Those other 980 people that essentially opted-in, saying that they were fans and willing to see posts that you made, never know if you posted something. Sure, there are ways around this: you can ask your fans to basically do a double opt-in by not only "liking" your page, but then to change their settings to "see this page first." You can also create posts that are highly shareable, so that if you can get those first twenty people to start commenting and sharing your post, Facebook will show it to another twenty people, then perhaps another twenty if it really starts to take off. But wouldn't it be nicer, and so much better for your business, if you could create a post and have all of your fans see it? And not only your fans, but people who you know would benefit from what you are sharing that are not (yet) your fans? You got it – give Facebook some of your money and they will make this happen. It's called advertising.

Advertising is certainly not new to digital marketing. People have been paying for exposure on the internet since the day it was created. It has certainly changed however. Rather than seeing pop-up ads, interruption ads, and fixed banners, today we live in a world of contextual and targeted ads. Both of these are important for your online business, whether you are an expert power blogger or a company selling goods and services. I've heard it said that amateur marketers do things like blog, SEO, and social media, while professional marketers pay for their leads with advertising, thus guaranteeing more and better results.

In an idealistic world, of course, everyone would love to be on page one of Google. Books have been written and even companies have been formed for what has become known as "Inbound Marketing," getting people to search for you rather, than you have to reach out to them (Outbound Marketing). The truth is, you need both.

Bob Kittell, internationally renowned award-winning speaker, tells a story of a young girl who had a lemonade stand. No one was coming to buy her lemonade, so she started going door to door to sell her lemonade. As she was down the street pouring lemonade into a neighbor's cup, her mother came up and asked her what she was doing, she replied, "Mom, the money's behind the doors!" That is why you need outbound marketing and not just inbound. The fact is, the money is behind the doors.

Contextual Ads

For our purposes, when we discuss contextual ads, I am going to talk about Google AdWords and AdSense. Basically, the way it works is that Google is constantly mining your data. When you do a search, of course Google knows what you just searched for, and they can display ads based upon what those search terms were. That is pretty straight forward. You are looking for an attorney, so Google shows you ads for attorneys, usually geographically-based results. Google calls this program AdWords, and you can sign up with Google, bid on what keywords you wish to rank for, and then upload your ads.

AdWords has gotten increasingly more sophisticated over the years, both in terms of how you can bid on various search terms, and the types of ads you can place. This includes both graphic ads and video ads on YouTube, as well as the standard text-based ads that you see in the search results. If you are advertising with Google, I highly recommend that you at least use graphic ads. The reason is that these ads are used for contextual based advertising, not just search results.

Google also looks at everything in context with what is on a page as well, and that page includes your email messages. If you are emailing your friends about going skiing (and you happen to be using a Gmail account), don't be surprised to see ads for ski gear showing up on your screen. That is the price of "free." Nothing is private. Google also uses contextual ads on blog pages. If you are reading an article about gardening, you may notice ads on the page about garden supplies. The site owner did not seek out the garden center and ask him to advertise on his or her page. Rather the site owner placed a small piece of code on his or her site that allows Google to match up relevant ads and display them on the page. Each time someone clicks on one of those ads, Google makes money, and they share a portion of that money with the site owner. As a blogger, this is another way to monetize your site. Google calls this program AdSense and it is geared towards content-rich sites like blogs.

I promised this was not going to be a technical manual. There are plenty of other books out there that show you specifically how you can do this, including The AdSense Code by my friend Joel Comm. This process is not difficult, and is something that I do with my Cyberbase Trading Post site. When you go there, you will notice two types of ads, Amazon affiliate ads and Google AdSense ads. The difference is that if someone clicks on the affiliate ads, I only get paid if they buy something. If someone clicks on an AdSense ad, I get paid a few cents just for them clicking on the ad. Be forewarned: if you click on AdSense ads on your own website, Google will look at this as a way for you to try to increase your revenue with fake clicks and will ban you FOR LIFE from the AdSense program. Don't do it!

While Google will try to match up ads that it presents based on the content of your pages, you can tell Google what types of ads you want to have displayed on your website. For example, on my Cyberbase site, which is geared towards Boy Scouts, I certainly don't want any "adult content" being shown there. I can also limit the ads from showing any competitors if I choose. I can also specify some general keywords, even if those don't show up in the content of the page (like camping for instance).

If you run an ecommerce store, you can see how huge this might be for you. When you create a contextual ad on Google, your ad doesn't just show up when someone searches for the keywords you are bidding on, but your ad will be displayed on all kinds of websites and blogs that are related to what you are selling. There are over 14 million AdSense-enabled websites, so your ad has the chance of being displayed to a very large audience and might even appear on big sites like CNN.com, Weather.com, or even other Google-owned sites including YouTube.

Targeted (& Re-Targeted) Ads

Contextual ads of course require that someone is searching for what you have to offer. For years, internet marketers insisted that this was the way of the new economy, and many "experts" trash-talked outbound marketing, primarily because it wasn't targeted. Today of course, you can easily target your advertising with digital ads. As Josh Kent, the CEO of Sun Frog Shirts says, *"The days of hoping that someone searches for a specific keyword and bringing them over to our site are over. It's a different world."* He is, of course, referring to Facebook advertising.

Like Google, Facebook has collected a ton of data about you – and this is all data that you have freely given them. When you signed up for a Facebook account, you told them your birthday (so they know how old you are), your sex, and where you live. So, they already have that demographic data about you. But then every time you post something on Facebook, they learn a little more about you, what your interests are, where you travel, and who your friends are. And they use this data to allow advertisers to target their ads based upon this information. And like Google, Facebook tracks your location with the GPS built into your phone – even if you don't have the Facebook app open. If you travel somewhere, or go into a particular store, Facebook knows about it. From a consumer standpoint, this sounds scary, but for a marketer, having access to the exact target audience you are trying to reach is incredible!

What this means for you as an advertiser, is that you can only show your ads to someone who is interested in what you have to offer. In addition to targeting ads by narrowing the characteristics of your buyer persona, you can create what Facebook calls a "custom audience." You need to have a minimum of two thousand emails to create a custom audience, which you then upload into Facebook, and Facebook will only show your ads to those two thousand people (assuming they have a Facebook account that uses that email address). You can take it a step further and have Facebook find people who have similar demographic data as your email list, thus allowing you to show your ads to people who are similar to your current customers.

The detailed targeting for your Facebook ads basically consists of three parts:

- Include people who meet at least one criteria, that you enter. This is similar to the "OR" operator.
- Exclude people from the above list, the "NOT operator.
- Narrow your audience, the "AND" operator.

So, you might include people who:

Have an interest in camping OR have an interest in hiking OR have an interest in backpacking AND who spend above average in online purchases AND who live within 50 miles of Denver, Colorado, but do NOT drive a Prius.

Once you have defined your audience, you can save it so that you can target future ads to the same types of people.

At this point, I must tell you about two basic types of "ads" that you can create with Facebook: a "Boosted Post" and a

"Newsfeed Ad." While they are similar in what they look like to the person viewing them, there are some key differences. Boosted Posts are pretty easy to create – just write a post and click on the "Boost Post" button. You do not have as many choices with a Boosted Post as you do with an ad, but you can do some limited targeting. The primary purpose of a Boosted Post is to get more "Likes" for your Facebook page, or "Event Responses," basically things that keep the user on Facebook. As a result, the cost of a Boosted Post is cheaper than an ad.

Elsewhere in this book, I talk about how your goal should be to get people off Facebook and onto your own list. You want to own your own destiny, not be "renting" it from someone else. Ads allow you to take people off of Facebook and offer them something to sign up for your email list. You do this by choosing "Traffic" as your advertising objective. Within the traffic objective, you now have two choices: send people to a website page, or send your ad to the Facebook messenger (chat). Both are pretty cool, and I like to run two similar ads, one to each.

As I write this, Facebook ads are the cheapest form of targeted advertising available. In fact, it is so cheap, I recommend that when you start an advertising campaign, that you experiment with your ads. I like to create a minimum of three ads per test. One might be a video ad, another a static image, and another a carousel of various images, or all three ads might be different static images. There is nothing that says you have to limit your test to just three ads. You can certainly do more. I then run all the test ads for forty-eight hours (2 days). This gives the ads enough time to see which one is the most effective. Once you determine which ad is going to perform the best, you can turn off the other ads and spend the rest of your money on the one that you know is going to have the biggest impact. This works so well, that for my clients who still do print ads, we run Facebook ads to test their artwork and copy, even if is then going to end up being used for a printed advertising campaign. This is a great way to test things out before you spend a lot of money on printing.

Because of the way that Facebook algorithms work, I do not recommend creating your test ads as part of the same campaign. Facebook has a feature that makes it super easy to upload bulk images to create several ads at once. They also have a feature to "create a similar" ad. Both of these methods build additional ads under the same campaign. But Facebook does not necessarily give them equal treatment and may show one of the ads more than the others. In order to get a more fair test to see which one is truly performing the best, do the extra work and create a separate campaign for each ad. Facebook may still show one ad more than the others, but at least you will know that all the ads have a fair shot at winning.

Facebook ads have another advantage as well: your ads don't just get displayed on Facebook. Facebook owns Instagram, so they display your ads on that platform as well, and your targeted audience still applies. They also have a network of other places where your ads might appear, even though they are outside of Facebook, including places such as Apple TV. This makes the case for advertising with Facebook even stronger.

Facebook has certain criteria for its ads, including a limited amount of text on the image associated with an ad or overlaid onto a video ad. You can add copy to your ad above the image, so it looks more like a post, but the image itself can't contain more than twenty percent text or Facebook might not show the ad. Some of the things I've found that make an effective Facebook ad include:

- **Relevancy**. For example, events, especially those that are related to certain holidays or current events are a good thing to advertise to get more attendance.

- **Visual**: Ads that include images of pets and children do especially well, but funny images or images with a wow factor also work well.

- **Shareable**: Sound familiar? Free offers that are widely desired and easy to reproduce make your ads shareable. People also like to share ads that contain great information and / or have great images.

- **Call-to-Action**: Your ads will perform better if they contain a very clear call-to-action. Since you are trying to get them off Facebook and onto your own website, the "Learn More" button is usually a safe bet. People often don't buy based upon seeing a single ad, so you should send them to a customized landing page that expands upon what you are offering in the ad. That custom landing page can contain the sales copy to get them to sign up for your emails and then continue to work them through an upsell process. I highly recommend that your ads go to a specific landing page, and not to the home page of your website. Bring them to a page that is relevant to what you are advertising. Don't try to advertise your store – advertise a specific product or event.

For example, I recently ran a set of ads for a client located in beautiful Estes Park, Colorado. Estes Park is a tourist town that sits at the base of Rocky Mountain National Park. My client had some lady's gloves that he wanted to advertise because it was autumn and the weather was getting cooler. His goal was to get people to drive up from Denver and visit his store. I don't know about you, but I probably wouldn't make a two-hour drive to buy a pair of lady's gloves, so I suggested that instead of focusing on the product, that we create a series of ads that showed why someone would want to come up to the mountains at this time of the year – the aspens were changing color, the elk were in rut (the mating season), and they would come down from the park and roam the streets of the town. There were lots of activities in the town including parades, concerts, and festivals. Get people to drive up to Estes Park to enjoy fall in the Rockies, then they could buy the gloves or anything else.

We ended up creating three ads: one with aspen trees (that also showed the ladies gloves to appease my client), one with a photo of the elk on the sidewalk outside of his store with a headline that said, "Come shop where the locals shop," and a third with a picture of the elk standing in the river just outside the back door of his store with a headline that read, "Watch the elk from our store." We tested all three ads against each other to see which one performed the best. I would have picked number two as the winner, but it was number three that got the most clicks, likes, comments and shares – by a large margin. The reason was because it met all of the criteria stated above. It was relevant, visual, shareable, and had a clear call-to-action (come and watch the elk from our store).

I've used this approach on a number of ads for different customers. For a maid-cleaning service, rather than creating ads showing pictures of maids, or even showing pictures of a clean house, I created ads that show a woman enjoying her time off by hiking, skiing, running, or otherwise enjoying the outdoors. The implication is that she has the free time to do what she enjoys because she isn't tied down to cleaning her home. The headlines usually read something like, "I have big plans for the weekend...cleaning the house isn't one of them." When you create an ad, always try to appeal to your customer's emotions rather than trying to sell a specific product or service.

Once your Facebook ads are working, you will want to convert them. Again, it is important that your ads send them to a custom landing page. As a general rule, simple landing pages are best. Your goal is to simply have the visitor give you their email address regardless of what you are selling. Once you have their email address, you can continue to market to them in the future. Your landing page should basically require someone to enter their email in order to claim your offer.

After the visitor has claimed your offer, you can try to upsell them on what you really want them to buy. This should be on "the other side" of the landing page. Refer to the copy I shared with you in chapter 7 about the fake candles.

What happens if someone clicks on your ad and doesn't enter their email? Rather than losing them forever, you can now go back and "re-target" them. Retargeting has actually been around for a number of years, but it has gotten increasingly easy to do thanks to both Facebook and AdRoll. Here's how it works:

Someone visits your site. It doesn't matter how they got there, but since this chapter is about advertising, we are going to assume that we drove them to the site from one of our ads. On the landing page (or product page), you insert a small piece of code that is referred to as a pixel. The retargeting pixel code gives instructions to the visitor's browser to request a one single pixel image from the retargeting company servers. The retargeting network uses the request to place a cookie on the visitor's desktop. For tracking each product seen at the product page level, a unique product ID (often a SKU) is generated with the pixel request. I like to put both the code from Facebook and the code from AdRoll on the landing pages as I use both of these networks to do retargeting.

Once someone has visited the page, your ads now follow them wherever they go on the internet. Let's say for example that Bob Jones clicked on your Facebook ad and ends up on your landing page. He does not enter his email, but instead closes your site without taking any action. A cookie has now been placed on his computer. Later that day he goes to dictionary.com and sees a horizontal banner ad, called a leaderboard, for your product or service across the top of that page. Then he goes to a local news site and there is a sidebar ad, called a skyscraper, along the right side of the page. Then he goes to a travel site later in the day and a square ad appears within the content of a blog post. Your ads are being shown everywhere he goes, even on huge nationally and internationally recognized sites.

You've seen this happen I'm sure. You visit Amazon and look at a product and then you start to see ads for that product on Facebook and lots of other places. But you don't have to be Amazon or have a huge budget to do this. You do, however, have to create all the various sizes of ads, because all the sites in the advertising network use different sizes to display ads. And, of course, you have to put the tracking pixel on the appropriate page on your website.

For Facebook, there is a single pixel that you place on your website. This is called the "base pixel" and you only install it one time, typically in the header part of your code, so that it appears on every single page of your website. If you want, you can stop there, but Facebook gives you a lot more power than that. They also provide you with "event codes" that allow you track specific actions including:

Website action	Standard event code
View content	fbq('track', 'ViewContent');
Search	fbq('track', 'Search');
Add to cart	fbq('track', 'AddToCart');
Add to wishlist	fbq('track', 'AddToWishlist');
Initiate checkout	fbq('track', 'InitiateCheckout');
Add payment info	fbq('track', 'AddPaymentInfo');
Make purchase	fbq('track', 'Purchase', {value: '0.00', currency: 'USD'});
Lead	fbq('track', 'Lead');
Complete registration	fbq('track', 'CompleteRegistration');

These event codes are placed on specific pages, such as the shopping cart page. You can also add different parameters for each standard event code, such as Content ID, value and currency. The conversion event requires value and currency parameters to work. Parameters are optional for all other standard events.

You can now create ads that are based upon the actions that someone took on your webpage. For example, if Bob Jones signed up for my premium certificate maker (he made a purchase), I might wish to show him a different ad (such as an ad for a custom frame), rather than offer someone who only used the free certificate maker. In that case, I might want to show him an ad for the premium version.

AdRoll, of course, allows you to track actions or events as well, but the process is a little bit different. First, you create a segment that will be associated with the event. Name the segment so that you can easily recognize it—for example, *Submit Form.*

Next, you find a link that reads "copy ID to clipboard" below the space where you entered your segment name. This pulls a unique numeric segment ID to be used as the URL rule placeholder for the segment you are creating (and later to prepare your script). Now, you will use this ID under Segment Type and Rule. Making sure that you've selected "URL" as the segment type, enter a "+" and then paste the segment ID number in the corresponding field. Enter your desired *Duration*—the number of days that the qualifying visitor should remain an active part of the segment.

AdRoll then gives you a script, called an event pixel, that you will need to tie the event in question to your event segment. Update the segment pixel by replacing the segment_ID in quotes with the unique segment ID generated for you.

If all this sounds like Greek or simply looks too hard, I can help. I've had a fair amount of experience with Facebook ads, to the point that Facebook has even asked for my advice about their advertising program. My business is designed to help you sell more online and make you successful on the internet. I would love to create an online marketing campaign for your company.

It may be that you are selling products on a site that you don't control, such as eBay or Amazon. Even some sites that you do control, such as Wix, don't allow you to place retargeting cookies on them. In that case, you can't track events, such as buying a particular item, because you have no way of adding the event pixels to someone else's website. Amazon doesn't give you access to the source code for their site, even if it is your product. However, I have figured out a way to add the basic tracking pixel if you want to do some simple retargeting. Here's how:

First, create a fake landing page on your website (that you do control). In the code, paste in the AdRoll code at the top of the page. Next add in an "if statement" or something to check to make sure that the cookie has been set. If it hasn't, return them to the AdRoll code until the cookie does get set. Once the cookie has been set, which only take a second or so, put in the code to re-direct the visitor to the Amazon page where the product is being sold. This method should work for any third-party site you might be selling on (including Wix websites).

Retargeting is important for you to consider, not just because you can get a customer to visit your page again, but also because it greatly improves brand recall. Even if a customer doesn't click on your ads, seeing them as they visit other websites places you as first in their mind. Retargeting is very good for pulling in new customers, but an added benefit is that it works on your existing customer base, as well. It keeps your name front and center in their minds, and reminds them to check for new products or updated services. It reinforces your brand, almost effortlessly.

I like to provide a phone number on the ads, so that it is easy for someone to contact me (or my clients), even if they don't click on the ad. Retargeting ads also allow you to stop fumbling for keywords. You no-longer have to be a mind-reader or speculate what kinds of things people are searching for to find services like yours, or what your ideal customer may be doing online when he's not on your site. He or she will tell you, just by landing on your page and leaving to do whatever they like. By being able to track that behavior, you can find out in great detail what your target demographic likes to do, where they like to go, and use that to reach them.

Retargeted ads can be useful for re-engaging lost shopping carts. Show images of one of the items left behind as a reminder. You can even link to a content page that more fully explains the benefit of the product. No matter what you choose to do, you're using the choices that visitor already made back in the forefront of his mind.

Retargeting actually stretches your marketing dollar. Studies show that only one in every 1,667 display ads gets clicked. Rather than thinking of this as another advertising expense, realize that a retargeted ad is up to 400% more likely to be clicked than a non-retargeted ad. But even when your ad is not clicked on, it is bringing brand awareness to the visitor.

In this world of information overload, it's often he who has the best brand awareness who "wins." By specifically targeting previous visitors with specific information that's tailored to his needs and interests, you win at branding. You reinforce your brand over and over until your business is what the customer thinks of when he thinks of your product or service. You gain a competitive edge with every ad that's displayed. That's priceless.

I covered a lot of information in this chapter, and I've shown you lots of ways to gain additional exposure through ads. The primary take-away is that I want you to leave with is that your ads should be used to collect emails. Selling is great, but collecting emails from people who click on your ads should be your primary goal. Once you have their emails, they are now on your list and you can market to them directly. Sending out automated emails is what we will cover in the next chapter.

Chapter 9 – Automated Emails

"Signing up is a powerful signal of intent to buy. Send them email until they do."

- Jordie van Rijn
Email Marketing Consultant

"The money is in the list," and this is true. This is where you will make your most revenue. One of the most successful Facebook advertising campaigns is to simply get people to sign up for your email list by offering them an incentive to do so. If you have a physical store, you should also give people an easy way to sign up for your email list. While it is never a good idea to purchase a list (simply because it doesn't work and the fact that it is considered SPAM), your marketing efforts should be geared towards getting people off social media and onto your own email list.

Yes, it's great to have a large social media following, and I use social media, especially Facebook and LinkedIn. But ultimately, you want these people on your email list. Relying on social media is like living in a rented apartment, you don't own the prospect. Facebook, LinkedIn, Twitter, or whoever can change the rules on you overnight or delete your account. Only by moving people off your social media accounts and onto your own list will enable you to control your own destiny. Having 1,000 or 100,000 followers on social media is not the same as having an email list of the same size. Most of the money I derive from the GEARS method ends up coming from my own email list.

Because all email programs are constantly monitoring the bounce rate of emails that you send out, as well as spam complaints, I highly recommend purchasing a program like "Atomic Mail Verifier." This program allows you to check your list of email addresses to make sure they are valid before you send out an email blast. Keep your list up to date, so that when you send out automated emails, it reduces your "unsubscribe" rate and guarantees better delivery rates.

Whenever I write a blog post, it is automatically sent out to my list as a newsletter. In fact, whenever I write a blog post, it is also automatically posted to my Facebook page. I write a post one time, and it gets posted to Facebook and sent out as an email newsletter. Pretty cool, right? Here's how I do this:

MailPoet is a WordPress plug that allows you to send out emails directly from your website without having to use a third-party provider like Constant Contact, aWeber, or MailChimp. With MailPoet you can create automated newsletters that get sent out at specified times whether it be once a month, one a week, or daily, whenever you want, as long as there is new content that has been published. In other words, if you don't write a blog post, there is nothing new to send out. But if you do write a blog post, the newsletter can be scheduled to go out, for example, only on the second Saturday of each month. I recommend keeping in touch with your list once a week.

It is not necessary to send out an automated newsletter every time you write a blog post. You can format your newsletters to only send content from specific categories. I have a category called "newsletter," so when I create a blog post that I want to send as an emailed newsletter, I simply check this category. If I create a blog post such as an automated blog post from the Amabot plugin as I discussed elsewhere in this book, this does not trigger a newsletter.

MailPoet offers the ability to format your newsletter exactly the way you want it. In my case, the header and the footer remain the same, but the date changes and the content changes. The images that appear also change, based upon the featured image for the blog post. And, you can have multiple blog posts per newsletter, each based on different categories.

In the case of Cyberbase Trading Post, anyone who signs up for my free certificate maker will see my blog posts in their email, even if they don't return to the site. I also include jokes and Scoutmaster minutes in the emails so they are not just a sales piece. But all of the reviews, with the affiliate links are also included. And of course, these are automatically posted to the Cyberbase Facebook page as well, with the affiliate links.

Notice that my emails, whether they come from Cyberbase Trading Post or my WebStores Ltd. site contain valuable content. They are not simply sales pieces. People do not want to subscribe to your email list to get inundated with you trying to sell them something. Give them content they can use. Then you will have earned the right to sell them something once a month or so.

There are lots of ways to post to multiple social media accounts at once with programs like HootSuite. The problem with this is that at least for Facebook, these are not considered native posts and they don't perform as well as publishing a post yourself. You can create automated native posts using a plugin called Microblog Poster. Microblog Poster is not plug-n-play. You must set up an app in Facebook to get it to work. This is about an eight-step process that gets a little technical, but it is well-documented. Once you do this, you never have to worry about it again – in fact it will publish old posts as well, not only to Facebook, but various other social media accounts you set up including:

- twitter.com - Auto post to your account.
- facebook.com - Auto publish to profile / page wall.
- plurk.com - Auto post to your account.
- delicious.com - Auto submit bookmark of your blogpost to your account.
- diigo.com - Auto submit bookmark of your blogpost.
- linkedin.com - Auto publish to profile wall.
- tumblr.com - Auto publish to your blog.
- blogger.com (blogspot.com) - Auto publish to your blog.
- instapaper.com - Auto submit bookmark of your blogpost.
- vk.com (vkontakte.com) - Auto publish to profile wall.
- xing.com - Auto publish to profile wall.
- pinterest.com - Auto publish to Pinterest board.
- flickr.com - Auto publish to Flickr.
- WordPress blog - Auto publish to another blog.

Most of those sites are not that common. Some like Twitter, will obviously not contain your full post. But the point is, you want to write your content once and then automate your tasks as much as possible to post to your social media accounts and send it to your newsletter subscribers. Do it once, then automate everything else.

Autoresponders

One aspect of automated emails that I haven't touched on yet is autoresponders. Autoresponders are messages set to go out automatically. They help you automate campaigns and manage one-to-one communication with your recipients.

Autoresponders are sent to your contacts in a sequence at intervals calculated starting from the day a contact opts into your campaign. For example, Day 0 (instant message), 3, 7, 14, 21. So, autoresponders are useful if you want to send an automatic message to contacts who join your list. This is known as a drip campaign. When you set up an autoresponder cycle, messages will go out on a specific day of a contact's subscription period. This, of course, is totally different than the automated newsletters I previously talked about.

The MailPoet plugin, I've mentioned before, has a limited drip campaign feature. You simply need to create multiple autoresponders at different intervals when someone signs up for your list. There is an add-on to WooCommerce (which I discuss later in the Revenue Chapter) that allows your customers to sign up when they check out of your store. You can have them sign up to a different list (such as "customers"), that will have a different sequence of autoresponders than the "subscriber" list email sequence.

Most email service providers like MailChimp, AWeber, and ConstantContact include auto-responder features. There are a few free autoresponders, including FreeFollowup.com. And certainly, there are other more sophisticated solutions like GetResponse, InfusionSoft, and AgileCRM that are worth considering. One thing you will want to consider is creating evergreen webinars (that is, you record the webinar once, then leave the replay up as if it is live). When people click on your webinar offer, you will want to take them through your series of autoresponder emails.

As with your automated newsletters the goal of an autoresponder is to make your business scalable.

Chapter 10 – Attend Live Events

"It's ironic, but true, that in this age of electronic communications, personal interaction is becoming more important than ever."

- Regis McKenna
Apple's First Marketing Guru

If you are selling low cost products, you may be able to sell items over the internet without ever having to meet your customers. But the quickest way to get someone to know, like and trust you, is to meet them in person. Regardless of what type of business you are in, ultimately you are in the relationship business. The best way to have a relationship with someone is to meet them in person. One of the most successful Facebook ad campaigns you can do is to promote your live events, rather than trying to sell a product or service, invite them to come to your free event!

A popular trend in innovative marketing is in-store events. During these promotions, retailers have an opportunity to build their community, highlight new merchandise and services, and sell an event along with their products. Offering attendees a memorable experience is an effective way to attract new customers and give existing ones a reason to return. I have a client that owns a new-age bookstore and she hosts events at her business every single week. Examples include classes and clinics, guest appearances, and seminars. Partner with your vendors to make your event stronger and promote the fact that a representative from the company will be on hand.

Recruit New Customers

To recruit new customers, you can use in-store events best suited to groups in order to enlist the help of your current audience. Events that invite people to linger over drinks or appetizers while previewing new products or learn a new skill are great ways to encourage your existing audience to bring their friends.

Clinics

This could be co-hosted at a school or public area other than the shop. Participants can be given a special coupon or vouchers for promo items (such as a lift ticket for a ski shop) when they come to the store.

Bring a Friend Special Shopping Night

Bring a friend and you'll both enjoy a special night. Get an extra X% off certain items, sit in on an introductory clinic, enjoy some free promotional gear and snacks.

Family Day

Set up a weekend day where there are resorts/travel agents there promoting family package deals, face painters or balloon makers, sticker and keychain style giveaways, raffles, etc.

Author Signings

You don't have to be a book store to host an author book-signing event. If you sell kitchen gadgets, host an author of a cookbook. If you sell pet supplies, host an author of a book on dog care.

Educate Your Audience

The more people know about your products and services, the more they'll want to take advantage of them. By offering free opportunities for education through special in-store events, you can encourage people to learn a new skill, expand their horizons, and open their minds (and their wallets) to new opportunities.

Q&A Seminar

Host a free info session on equipment and trip planning.

Summer Storage Clinic

If you have a ski shop, learn how to clean, wax and store your ski and snowboard equipment until next season. Get free wax, extra XX% off spring clearance coupon, and refreshments!

Multi-Week Classes

Hold a series of classes over several weeks, say every Wednesday night. For example, if you are a yarn shop, hold a class on knitting. If you sell kitchen gadgets, offer a gourmet cooking class.

Customer Clinics

A great way for staff to practice their product tech knowledge and showcase new tech to customers at the same time.

Create Loyal Clients

Invite-only in-store events are a great way to single out your best customers and reward them for their loyalty. These special VIP events can include sneak peeks at new products, a first look at special sales, and a yearly party to show your gratitude. Anything you can do to celebrate the people who are the core of your business is a great way to say thank you.

VIP / Sneak Preview Event

Hold events for frequent/past customers, after hours.

VIP First Dibs Clearance Event

Before spring clearance is made live, invite your VIPs, Facebook Community, etc. for "first dibs" on clearance preview.

Women's Only Preview & Wine Tasting

Women love to be pampered and are important product purchasers as they buy for their family and significant others in addition to their own gear.

Give Back to the Community

In-store events aren't just about getting new customers and making sales, they're also about giving back. Partner with other businesses or community organizations to offer promotions, educational opportunities, or DIY projects to underserved communities or non-profit organizations. These events can help your business reach new audiences while earning you karma points.

Cookie Sales

Customers bring in a tray of cookies and receive discount off one item. Cookies are donated to shelters – a great deed that also brings great local PR and evokes a great feeling about your business.

Animal Swap

One of the most brilliant events I've seen is hosted by one of my customers that owns a feed store. Each Spring and Fall, they host an animal swap in their parking lot – people bring their kittens, bunnies, puppies or whatever to give away for free. Of course, the new pet owner now has to buy feed and supplies, which happens to be conveniently located next to the parking lot. This is also a great community get-together.

Let Others Use Your Space

Meet Ups are very popular groups about all sorts of interests. The problem that many Meet Up groups have is finding a space to meet. Rather than forcing them to go to a local coffee shop or library, why not make your space available to them? If you have a swim shop for example, let swim teams meet at your location. Not only is this a great community service, but this is a great way to bring new customers into your store. You may find this is a better use of your square footage than filling every nook and cranny with more merchandise.

Maximize Your Sale

Everyone loves a good sale. This means hosting an opportunity to save money is a great way to excite your community. Don't relegate clearance items to a hard-to-find rack or shelf in the back of your store. Instead, throw a party for your end-of-season items and give them the send-off they deserve right at your store's entrance.

Sidewalk Sale

Springtime has the perfect weather to host outdoor sales to attract attention of passers-by, in addition to those in your informed customer community.

Combined with music, food and other businesses this can boost your inventory turnover at the end of the season!

Shred Betty Sale / Sportsman's Sale

A weekend of discounts only on women's / men's snowboard hard and softgoods. Includes brunchy appetizers each morning, a clinic taught by a female / male, and a raffle for a women's / men's snowboard video.

Making virtual waves

In-store events happen IRL (In Real Life), but they don't stop there. Create buzz before the event and expand its reach with the help of social media campaigns, hashtags, and behind-the-scenes photos. Continue to promote the event after-the-fact with photos, stories, and customer testimonials.

GOAL: Recruit New Customers

Develop a hashtag unique to your event and invite guests to share their photos on social media. This will give you a variety of user-generated content to use during your event and long after it's over.

GOAL: Educate Your Audience

Create how-to and instructional YouTube videos. You can embed these high-value videos on your website and share them across social media channels as a sneak peek to your event and for customers to access 24/7.

GOAL: Create Loyal Clients

Develop a customer loyalty program. This is a great way to incentivize return customers and can be as simple as signing up for an exclusive email list or as elaborate as offering reward points for purchases.

GOAL: Give Back to the Community

Leverage the power of live streaming. Sharing live video footage during your philanthropic event will expand both your reach and your efforts to the entire social community.

There are also events that are hosted by others that allow you to meet your customers. These might include:

Conferences

Most professions host a variety of conferences throughout the year. These are typically multi-day events where you can mingle with the other attendees in the evenings. Often, these are not inexpensive, as the conference fees, hotels, and airfares add up, not to mention the time away from work. However, they can be a goldmine for your business if you really go there to network and not just soak up what the speakers have to offer. The expense can be well worth it, and I recommend that everyone attend at least one conference a year.

Seminars

Seminars are like a conference that only lasts for a couple of hours. These are usually local, so they are a lot less expensive.

Digital versions of seminars (webinars) do not have the advantage of having the opportunity to meet the other attendees or the speakers. It's important to get out and meet people. It should be easy to attend half a dozen seminars during the course of a year.

Trade Shows

Yes, trade shows still exist. Sometimes a trade show is held in connection with a conference, other times shows are the main attraction. Vendors pay a lot of money to exhibit at certain shows and they want to talk to you. It is sad to go to a show and the vendor is reading a book or working on his or her computer and are not engaging with participants. Don't be afraid to talk to the vendors. They aren't usually trying to sell you something on the spot, but to educate you about their products. So, go learn something and have fun.

Meet Ups

Meet Ups were started after 9-11 as a way to get people to engage socially on a local level. Today there are thousands of Meet Ups in most communities covering a huge array of interests. This is a great way to meet like-minded people. You could probably go to a different Meet Up every day, or certainly once a week, and I recommend that you find those that interest you and go at least once a month. Better yet, if you are a business and have a meeting space, why not host a Meet Up based on a topic that is relevant to your customers? Go to MeetUp.com to find out more.

Remember, the goal of hosting or attending live events is not to make sales, it is to meet with your customers and establish a know, like, and trust relationship. Once you have trust and have established your expertise, the sales will naturally follow. If you are looking to host your own live event, here is some additional advice.

HOW TO CREATE A LIVE EVENT … AND WHY YOU SHOULD BY JUDITH BRILES

Creating a Live Event and doing them on an ongoing basis creates Super Fans for you and whatever you are selling and represent. You become an influencer of

The Why …

Hot spit … you have generated a following—FANS—a tribe of individuals who connect with you via email or one of your social media platforms. They look forward to sage advice, your zany sayings and quotes … and they want more. Meaning YOU … a day or a few with just you … or maybe you and a few others who could add to their knowledge base.

The Should …

Using your expertise to enhance followers and followers-to-be is a smart thing to do. Having face-to-face time with you that an onsite live event does; and to experience you and your wisdom can turn the most casual of followers into a Raving Fans, or what is known amongst authors as Super Fans. Super Fans

142

become your marching marketers—they shout out through their own social media streams that you and your products are the best of the best. Buy them.

The How …

Are you ready? And if you are game … where do you start? What are the must haves that need to be in place? All good questions. As someone who has created from scratch live events for both small and large groups, it's an ongoing learning experience. I've done my own where it's "just me" and I've done events that include over 20 over speakers. I've done them "in person" using an offsite location … "at sea" using a cruise ship … in "my offices" using my outside deck, inner offices or my great room … and "online" where attendees are a click away. I've done them for a "free admission" and for "paid". And I've done them with "exhibitors" … who pay to be there. In other words, you've got options.

People like to connect. Whatever your theme is for the event … it's where like-minded attendees come together. Make sure you allow for that to happen. Your live event will be about education of your given topic. You've got to figure out how to reach out and connect with attendees for the invite; how to continue the connection once they are there; and what you are going to do in the follow-up mode.

You need to know your timing—when do you announce; if there is a fee, will you have early bird and late bird registration fees? What take-aways do you want attendees to embrace? What technology and presentation site will you need? Will it be a water only event or will you have food? Will you have handouts that need printing or will you supply online, leaving it up to the attendee after registration to download?

Live events are about engagement. With you. For online events, there may be engagement if set up ahead of time with attendees and guest speakers. You can create an open mic time for questions or take them via a chat box and respond. For in-person events, schmoozing and networking is a given. At my June three-day Judith Briles Book Publishing Unplugged event, I limit the number of participants to under 50. Meals are included, as is a detailed workbook. There are plenty of activities that have attendees moving around and interacting. Authoring and Publishing can be a lonely number—one of my goals for the Unplugged event is to seed a community of like-minded authors who desire success.

Tips to Rock Your Live Event

1. *Start with the topic.* You are the Thought Leader in putting it together. Is it around your expertise ... or is it around others and you are the planner, coordinating speakers and agenda? For me, I always stay with what I know—my expertise—book publishing and working with authors. For my Judith Briles Book Publishing Unplugged and Judith Briles Speaking Unplugged, it's me. For the AuthorUExtravaganza.org and PublishingAtSea.com, I have a team of publishing pros that will be deliver workshops dedicated to author,

marketing and publishing success.

2. *Determine how you want to deliver your event.* There are a variety of formats designed for a handful of attendees; a select number or an unlimited. Some are over the phone; some via a computer; some using YouTube; some via live streaming; and some in person. You may prefer one way or mix them up.

- **Webinars** can be *info only*, *pitch oriented* for a product or service you offer or a *combo*. Webinars are online events.

- **Pick My Brain** or **Topic Teleconferences** highlights your expertise and can be *info only*, *pitch oriented* for a product or service you offer or a *combo*. Use one of the "free" conference services to reduce your costs—which is primarily your time in gathering participants.

- Multi-hour public or invitation only **Workshops** can be *info only*, *pitch oriented* for a product or service you offer or a *combo*. They can be online or in-person.

- Multi-day event **Workshops** or **Conferences** can be *info only*, *pitch oriented* for a product or service you offer or a *combo*. They can be online or in-person.

- Weekly or Monthly **Meetups** can be *info only, pitch oriented* for a product or service you offer or a *combo.* Setting up a Meetup.com group is uncomplicated; you are the organizer and therefore control the content and "rules" for inclusion (which could include a fee); and Meetup announces the formation of your group to already existing participants of like-minded members of its community and new members start to join. The magnet is the key words you use to describe what your group is about.

- Facebook Live and Google Hangouts can launch you on **Live Streaming** and transition to a posting on your YouTube channel.

3. *Your initial task is to connect with attendees and get them registered.* Are they coming from your lists only? What about "like" groups on Meetup.com? Do you have partners/affiliates who will be shouting out to theirs and you pay a commission or affiliate fee to them if anyone registers through their links? Are you going to be doing ads, such as on Facebook or Google? Will you be doing a special social media campaign around it? Or webinars? What about pushouts on your blog or being featured on a podcast?

   How are you going to keep track of registrants—an Excel spread sheet; using email management tools like

Aweber or Mail Chimp; or something else. The names and emails will be an essential part of your future marketing.

Mistakes commonly made are to be thinking every presentation has to be all new. You can incorporate information shared previously. Do add new items and rework what you've done with a twist. Repurposing is your friend.

4. *Don't Underestimate Social Media* – it's your Town Hall Shout Out. For every event I do, there is a special social media stream of posts for Facebook, Google+, LinkedIn, Twitter and a Pinterest board. Blogs are created plus a special email blast to all within out contact database.

   As the Early Bird deadline approaches, we use a "count down" – In 3 days ... in 2 days ... in 1 day ... Final Day to Save Money (or put an actual amount—in my case it was $150). Putting a "clock" on your registration will add to your success and the potential attendees' urgency reflex.

   On your Events tab (create one on your website), create a special page with more details, add images that relate to your event and topic. If you have already held one, add quotes from past attendees and images. You will have a "buy" button, make sure site info for the event is included and a phone number that an interested visitor could call and get more information.

What you want is a wide net. And to assist you, you want some type of a social media management tool, such as Hootsuite, so that you can set up massive postings over a period of time ... and then check it off your To Do list.

5. *Set your budget and determine what your will charge.* Or, you could do a freebie. No matter what, there will be some type of minimal charge. Ideally, you will make money. The savvy event giver will research what others are doing in topic area. If you are the "go to" expert ... you can set the pricing.

6. *Turn your participants into participants before your Event starts.* A pre-survey can be a goldmine of info for you to include "adds" to your event that you hadn't thought of. Typically, you will post an Agenda or bullets of all the items you will explore during your event. Create a "Tell me about YOU" survey—you can deliver it as each person registers, or you can do it in mass, such as after the Early Bird registration ends or even a few weeks before the big day. Ask what their goals are and/or why they are attending. Tools are readily available for both online poll taking as well as onsite that participants can access via their mobile.

Companies like EventMobi.com create mobile survey and polling tools that you can test on a free trial.

7. *Tap into a sponsor who can underwrite some of your costs.* Events cost money. Online ones that consist of a teleseminar or a webinar are on the low end. Once you get away from your offices, moneys can flow. Site costs, audio tech needs, printed material and food can run into the thousands. Your sponsor could already be in your circle as a member or a vendor who supplies product or services for the type of individual you are targeting.

   Sponsorship can come in "soft" and "hard" dollars. A radio show or podcast may want to feature you, even run an ad for your event. A vendor may want to add some swag to give away to attendees—you don't need it, but it's a perk for all. You don't have to pay for it. That's soft. Hard dollars pay for must haves—moneys toward room, printing, audiovisual, food, etc., costs. Sponsors want "something" –it could be a "live" commercial at your event, a booth to set up, ads in workbooks, special flyers given to all attendees, a blog about services—options are unlimited.

8. *Build momentum.* Get the buzz started. Create ongoing blogs, social media postings. Identify a hashtag that will be unique to you … and identify top hashtags for your topic to include in posts as you build up and during the event. Encourage attendees to post out about the event pre, and during, using them.

9. *Have fun.* Yes, this is work and when it's over, you could be exhausted. Plan on a treat for yourself.

10. *Post your event, follow up with attendees.* Make sure you do a post analysis—with yourself; with your staff if you have one; with your attendees. What worked; what didn't; what changes and/or adds are desired for your next that event.

    You will have emails, survey them for feedback. If you are doing a registration event or an event that people just showed up—get emails for all; create a customized link use a resource such as Bit.ly or TinyURL using your name or a word that the attendees will connect with your event and encourage them to go to it and receive a bonus or something special. Ask what steps are they going to take post your event.

And congratulations.

Judith Briles

The Book Shepherd, Book Publishing Expert, Author, Radio Host
How to Avoid 101 Book Publishing Blunders, Bloopers & Boo-Boos
Judith Briles Book Publishing Unplugged, Judith Briles Speaking Unplugged

http://TheBookShepherd.com

R: The Ring Gear - Results

"The great thing about fact-based decisions is that they overrule the hierarchy. The most junior person in the company can win an argument with the most senior person with a fact-based decision."

- Jeff Bezos
Founder and CEO of Amazon

FOREWORD by Joel Comm

We've all heard the mantra, know-like-trust. Like me, know me, trust me, pay me – it has to be done in that order. That brings us to this section of Greg's book: Results. This is the culmination of the previous sections, where he has discussed getting others to market on your behalf. And that is important. Marketing should tell a story so compelling, others want to retell it. Your customers are talking to you, telling you who they are, how they feel and what they need. With the right approach, you can make it a conversation.

Here's the thing: You are NOT in the business of selling a product or service. You are in the business of SERVING PEOPLE with the value that your product or service delivers. Without people, whose problems are solved with your product or service, you have no business.

When you put your attention on the people you are serving and how their lives will be enriched by giving you their money, your priorities are in the right place. With few exceptions, the relationships you have with others will determine how successful you are in your business. Success can be measured in a variety of ways, including revenues, visitors, and social interactions. As Greg points out, these need to be reviewed so you can repeat your successes (and avoid the things that aren't working).

Looking to the future by researching new opportunities is one way to insure your success over the long-term of your business.

As a futurist, this is an area that not only fascinates me, but one that I believe is important for any business to really look at and see how certain trends and technologies will impact their business in the coming years.

Clearly, live video is the most significant development in social media since the invention of the smartphone. It is the biggest move forward into making us more social. From 2015 to 2016 we moved from pioneer to early adopter phase and we now have a lot of people that are doing live video, but the masses have still not arrived. We're on the early part of the curve still. That's why I'm excited to talk about what I believe is coming to us next.

It's been interesting that as the power is shifting from traditional mainstream broadcasting to the citizens to you, you don't have to be a big brand, you don't have to be a major broadcaster to do a live video, what you do have to do is create content that is compelling so that people watch, and not only do they watch but they come back for more, and not only do they come back for more but they tell their friends. That is really the essence of viral marketing, telling a story so compelling that others will want to tell it for you.

Here is one of my predictions: Virtual reality and 360 video is going to move from pioneering to early adopter in 2017. It is the next phase. Of course, with 360 video we're talking about consumer grade versions of cameras. Facebook has the ability for you to upload 360 videos and then you can click around, and you can drag, and you can basically see anywhere. What we're looking for are experiences that put us in the center of the action. What we're wanting in business is to be able to draw our clients into the experience, for example, realtors, travel bureaus, these types of things, really anything where you want to show people behind the scenes and provide an experience for them.

Now, guess what? Here's your chance. Are you going to take it?

Joel Comm
Live Video Marketing Expert • Author • Speaker • Consultant • Brand Influencer • Futurist
NY Times Best-Selling Author
http://JoelComm.com

Chapter 11 – Revenue

"There is only one boss. The customer. And he can fire everybody in the company from the chairman on down simply by spending his money somewhere else."

- Sam Walton
Founder of WalMart

Your opinion doesn't matter. Only the customer's opinion matters and they are the ones that drive your most important metric - revenue.

Unlike a traditional marketing funnel, revenue is the biggest gear in my system, not the smallest part. This system is based on your number one priority and that is to convert traffic into paying customers.

Revenue generation from a website is one of the most confusing aspects to many web site owners. In large part, this is because it took over a decade for it to become easy enough for the average business owner to implement. PCI (payment card industry) compliance and security are still a concern, but it is now possible for anyone to have an ecommerce website. In this chapter. I'll discuss what you need to know to accept payments on your web site.

PCI compliance

The **Payment Card Industry** Data Security Standard (**PCI DSS**) is a proprietary information security standard for organizations that handle branded **credit cards** from the major card companies including Visa, MasterCard, American Express, and Discover. The PCI DSS applies to ANY organization, regardless of size or number of transactions, that accepts, transmits or stores any cardholder data. This used to be a major issue for small companies wanting to sell online. In fact, it was not really feasible to be PCI compliant. With the hosted payment solutions available today, it is no longer necessary for you to take credit card payments on your site directly. The credit cards can be entered directly into the merchant accounts and they are the ones who handle the liability. I'll talk more about this in a minute.

HTTPS / SSL

The terms SSL, TLS and HTTPS are often used interchangeably. They are not the same, but for the purposes of running an ecommerce website, we most often just hear and use the term SSL.

Secure Sockets Layer (SSL) is a cryptographic protocol that enables secure communications over the internet. SSL was originally developed by Netscape and released as SSL 2.0 in 1995. A much-improved SSL 3.0 was released in 1996.

Transport Layer Security (TLS) is the successor to SSL. TLS 1.0 was defined in January 1999. The differences between TLS 1.0 and SSL 3.0 were significant enough that they did not interoperate. Current browsers support TLS 1.0 by default and may optionally support TLS 1.1 and 1.2. Most business owners still simply refer to everything as an SSL certificate. This is fine, as SSL certificates issued today use TLS.

Hyper-Text Transfer Protocol Secure (HTTPS) is the secure version of HTTP, the protocol over which data is sent between your browser and the website that you are connected to. The 'S' at the end of HTTPS stands for "Secure." It means all communications between your browser and the website are encrypted. HTTPS is often used to protect highly confidential online transactions like online banking and online shopping order forms. If you have an SSL certificate installed on your site, you will be able to use https with your site.

Here's the main idea. You need an SSL certificate if you are going to sell online. SSL certificates used to be very expensive. An inexpensive SSL certificate is technically identical to a five hundred dollar SSL certificate. The difference is in the amount of insurance that you choose. If you are selling millions of dollars online and using your own servers, you may need a five hundred dollar certificate, but if you are using a hosted payment solution, where you are not storing credit card numbers yourself, you can opt for an entry level SSL certificate.

PayPal

PayPal was the original hosted payment solution. PayPal has an inherently different business model than traditional merchant account providers. Failing to understand this difference has caused many entrepreneurs to lose lots of money. The "risk" is involved when accepting credit cards such as Visa, MasterCard, and other card brands that give consumers six months from the final point of delivery to dispute a charge on their card. What this means is that at any point, up to six months after you sell a product, you may get a dispute (a "chargeback") and the money from that sale may be automatically pulled from your bank account. If you go out of business and your bank account can't be drafted for the refund, the merchant account provider (i.e., PayPal) refunds the customer.

PayPal (and Stripe) are what are considered merchant account "Aggregators". Instead of issuing a single merchant account to a single business, PayPal has ONE merchant account that they let millions of people use (it's a bit more complicated than that, but that is the basic idea). This model works because they are balancing the risk among millions of entrepreneurs and customers before people ask for refunds.

As a result of this many-to-one business model, PayPal is the easiest way to accept payments online. You can set this up in less than an hour. The disadvantage is that when you use it, the visitor leaves your website and enters their payment information on the PayPal site. This removes most of the liability from you, but it does not make the transaction seamless for the customer.

160

Still, I believe every website that sells online should accept PayPal as a payment solution. The reason is that some people, myself included, keep a certain amount of money in their PayPal account and use it to make online purchases. PayPal can be set up for anyone to use their credit card, even if they don't have a PayPal account, but most people find this cumbersome. The primary use for PayPal is for people like me who keep money in their PayPal account to make it easy to purchase things online. You want the ability to accept a customer's money in the way that is most convenient to them, not to you.

Stripe

Stripe is the savior for the small business owner. Like PayPal, it is a merchant account aggregator (using a many-to-one model). But, unlike PayPal, it allows you to take credit cards on your website without people leaving your site. As such, you must have an SSL certificate installed on your site, but it makes it really easy to get paid online just like the big boys. Stripe combines a traditional merchant account to receive funds and a gateway to submit payments into a single, simple solution.

There are other payment solutions out there that compete with Stripe, such as Braintree and Square. These payment methods have made it easy for small businesses to have a totally PCI compliant website without a lot of technical setup. Unlike PayPal, Stripe can be set up to transfer money to your bank account on a regular basis, so you don't have to login and manually transfer money. You will want to be sure to set up automated withdrawals. If you use manual transfers and don't take the money out, Stripe returns the money to the customer.

With an aggregate payment provider like Stripe, you can't accept cards that are physically swiped at your store at a point-of-sales terminal. This means that your processing fees will be higher for each transaction because of the higher security risk posed by an online payment. Currently the cost is 2.9% plus 30 cents per transaction.

Merchant Accounts

If you accept credit cards in your physical store, you likely have a merchant account. Unfortunately, this cannot be used with your online store without a separate approval process. If you are looking to get lower rates on your payment processing fees than what is offered by a payment aggregator, you will have to set up an online merchant account. This is a significantly more complex process and costs more to get setup and configured. Unless you are selling millions online, start with an all-in-one solution like Stripe. The application and setup costs of your own merchant account don't justify the lower fees you might pay, especially when you consider that you may need custom programming to get it to work.

Shopping Carts

There are lots of shopping cart solutions available today. Most are simple to setup and use. Be forewarned that none of them will meet all of your needs. I use WooCommerce, BigCommerce, Magento, Shopify, ECwid, and a host of others for my clients. They all have their own advantages and disadvantages and may not do exactly what you are looking for. At the same time, it is easier than ever to get started selling online, especially if your needs are that of a traditional retail shop.

WooCommerce is an ecommerce plugin for WordPress websites. If you have a WordPress website, this is the shopping cart you should be using. WooCommerce has a serious advantage over other shopping carts when it comes to designs. What I mean is that you can basically make any WordPress theme work with the platform, and there are thousands of WordPress themes on the web. WordPress allows you to create a website that performs all sorts of functions that a shopping cart-only solution doesn't provide. For example, if you are doing online bookings for a rental unit, there are plugins for that. If you need to sell memberships, have multiple pricing schemes, or connect to a point-of-sale system, there are numerous plugins for each of those. For example:

Pricing by Roles

Pricing by roles is an add-on to WooCommerce that allows you to set up roles such as distributors, resellers, non-profits, fundraisers, and event planners. Each role can be assigned a different price for each product in your online store. This makes it possible to turn WooCommerce into a wholesale shopping cart platform.

Membership Sites

Take a look at most successful ecommerce websites such as Amazon. They all have a means of generating recurring revenues, where customers pay you monthly, yearly or at other intervals. For Cyberbase Trading Post I use a plugin called Paid

Membership Pro. Another plugin called MemberPress is integrated with Affiliate Royale, so this may be the solution you want to use. But having a membership program for your most loyal customers should be a priority for any site that is using multiple revenue sources to generate income on the web.

Security

A major concern for anyone collecting money online should be security. There are a variety of WordPress plugins for making your site more secure, but you must realize that nothing is fool-proof. WordFence and iThemes Security are two good choices. But one of the best things you can do is to use unique, secure passwords.

One argument people use all the time is that they can't possibly remember a long, unique, secure password. Here's how you can make passwords easy to remember:

Create a saying, such as "You won't be late if you forget to smell the roses!" Change all the S's to $. Change the L's to 1. Use 2 instead of to. Use 4 instead of for. Use 8 instead of ate. Use 0's for O. And substitute 3 for E's. You might end up with something like this:

Uwon'tB3L8IfU4get2$m311TheRO$3$!

But you don't even have to remember all of this. There are programs out there like KeePass that will store hundreds of passwords in an encrypted file so you can simply copy and paste your passwords as you need them. Take your security seriously and use one of these programs.

Closing the Sale

One of the ongoing discussions I see regarding selling on the internet is what to do with the customer after he or she has put something into their shopping cart. There are those who insist that you should leave the customer on the page where they are, in order to make it easier for them to keep shopping. The problem is that the customer may not realize that they actually put the item in the shopping cart and click on the add-to-cart button multiple times, thereby adding the same item several times. They may get frustrated and leave because the shopping cart is not displayed to them.

Others will insist that it is better to display the shopping cart contents every time someone adds a product to the cart. That way the customer can easily visualize exactly what they are purchasing. Website visitors are not the most online savvy people around. To get them to select something else on the menu, these sites may have a "continue shopping" button that either takes them back to the last page they were on, the last category being viewed, or to the home page of the site.

Amazon uses a hybrid approach that seems to work well. When you add something to the cart, the cart contents are displayed, but so are a bunch of other related products that you might want to purchase as well. Since this method works well for the biggest ecommerce site on the internet, you might want to consider copying this method for your own site.

Be sure to make your checkout system as simple as you possibly can. Unless there is a compelling reason (such as a brand-new wholesale customer), don't make the person fill out a registration form to complete a sale. Shipping still remains a big concern for online vendors and customers alike. It is a proven fact that free shipping closes more sales. Unless you are selling tractors, swimming pools, or other large items that have to be shipped via a semi-truck, I highly recommend that you provide **free shipping**. One of the reasons why the Amazon Prime program is so successful is because it offers free shipping. You are competing with that whether you realize it or not. So, build the cost of shipping into your products and then tell your customers that you offer free shipping. In fact, mention it on every single product page. Bare minimum, provide free shipping if a customer orders a certain minimum dollar amount. Test this and see if it makes a difference in the number of sales you close.

Another thing that flies in the face of what most website designers will tell you is to offer more than one call-to-action on a page. Most designers will tell you to keep your interface clean and simple, giving your customers only one choice, to add the item to the shopping cart. Once again, Amazon does not follow this advice. Instead, they give you multiple call-to-action options on any given page, whether it be to add a product to the cart, save it to a wish list, compare other higher price items (an upsell), add-on products (a cross-sell), look at competing products, or even to click on an ad from an external website. Amazon sells more than the people giving you the advice to only have a single call-to-action on your page. It's like the basic sales principle of giving the customer the illusion that they are in control when you tell them you have free time on Tuesday evening or Thursday morning. Which one works better for them? You gave them a choice to say yes between option A and option B, just not to say no. The choice is yours, but I'd rather copy the winning strategy and offer upsells and cross sell items on my page.

Generating more revenue and closing more sales on your website is not just a matter of getting the technology in place however. It is not simply a matter of designing your website to keep the customer shopping and adding more items to their cart. Those things are important, but are not what makes a customer decide to purchase from you rather than someone else. A huge factor in closing the sale comes from the photographs, videos, and written copy that is presented to them. I covered most of this in "Chapter 7 – Earn Even More".

Here are some things you can do to establish your site as the one where they want to spend their money.

1. Urgency
   One of the most reliable tools for closing sales is to create urgency. We all know that if a buyer puts off a buying decision, the opportunity to close the sale is typically lost for good. Give them a reason to buy now.

2. Authority
   Authority figures in our society play an important role in influencing behavior. This is an aspect where you can totally out-shine Amazon or most other sites on the

internet. Besides your weekly blog posts that establish you as an authority, consider using video as a way to communicate with your customers on the product pages. Create a video sharing your knowledge about a product, and talk to the customer in much the same way as you would if he or she walked into your store and inquired as to why they should buy that product.

3. Limited-Time Gift with Purchase
   Bonuses are also a great way to close sales. Many times, affiliates and joint venture partners will sweeten the pot when selling someone else's products by adding their own bonuses if you purchase before a certain date. Sometimes a personal motive can have a stronger impact on a buying decision than tools like price, free shipping or payment terms.

4. Referrals
   91% of customers say they'll give referrals, but only 11% of salespeople ask for referrals.   (Source: Dale Carnegie). And, according to the Journal of Marketing, a referred customer is 18% more loyal than a customer acquired through a different method and spends 13.2% more than a non-referred customer. As we've discussed throughout this book, word-of-mouth is the strongest form of marketing out there. If you can automate the referral process by giving your customers an incentive to recommend a friend while checking out, you can greatly improve your closing ratio. Consider combining this with one of the other methods described above,

such as "share this on Facebook" and we'll give you a free gift (or free shipping).

5. Follow Up

   After the sale is just as important as before the sale, yet many vendors completely stop once the sale is made and the product is shipped. In fact, this is so rare, that if you do a Google search for "follow up after the sale is made," ninety-nine percent of the results refer to "following up in order to close a sale" and not what to do after the sale is made. And most of the references to saying thank you after a sale is made are related to real estate agents. Here is an opportunity for you to stand out from the competition. When you ship your product, include a free (unexpected) gift with their order. Write a personal note thanking them for their business, then attach a coupon for their next order. I had one client that did this and asked them to review the product they just purchased. The coupon wasn't valid until the purchaser had written a review. It didn't matter if it was a positive or a negative review, he just wanted their opinion. Another time he did a similar thing by asking for referrals. Once the customer had given an identical coupon valued at 20%, to someone else they thought would enjoy his store, their coupon was activated. The result was that he grew his email list to over 70,000 in just a couple of years.

   Think about it. When was the last time you got a hand-written message in a package, even if it was just a computer font to look like handwriting that read something like this:

"I just wanted to send you a note of thanks for your recent order. New clients are the lifeblood of our business. I hope you are enjoying your new printer.

Let me show my appreciation by offering you a special offer. For the next 90 days, if you need any ink cartridges or paper, I'll give you 1 extra FREE for every 2 you buy.

Buy 2 and Get 1 Free!

There's no limit on this offer as long as you purchase during the next 90 days. The reason I'm making you this offer is to get you into the habit of ordering your supplies from us. I know that once you've shopped here a few times, you'll want to order from us over and over again. We want pleased customers.

Should you have any concerns or issues with your order, call me at 555-1234.

Thanks again for your business. It has been a pleasure serving you and I look forward to an ongoing relationship."

I read a blog where an auto-mechanic had sent out a hand-written note to his customers after working on their car. The note wasn't long, it simply read: *"Thank you for allowing us to work on your car. I truly appreciate your business and I hope that you were satisfied with the level of service we provided. Please don't hesitate to call on us again."*

The person receiving the service was appreciative enough that he scanned the note and posted it on the internet. One of the comments to his post read:

"It's little things like this that earn business. If I got this card I would never use another mechanic in my life."

By simply saying thank you, you're doing something most businesses don't bother with. That sets you apart from the herd.

Besides adding in a coupon or free gift to the package itself, don't forget to send out at least three follow up emails – one notifying them that the package was shipped (along with a tracking number if you have it). Two, about a week later, to make sure they got the package, and three, about two weeks after that to make sure they are satisfied with their purchase. If they are happy with their purchase, could they please provide a product review (with the link to the product to make it easy for them)? Of course, when they click on the product link, they see other cross-sells and up-sells!

Whatever your method, it's important to say thanks after making a sale as part of making it a good experience for your client.

Once you set up all the things we've discussed in this chapter, you will be able to collect revenues for your business in a safe, secure way. You will be getting paid on a regular basis. And you will be closing more sales. If you are being successful, you need to find out what is working so you can repeat the process over and over again. That is what we will talk about in the next chapter – review and repeat.

Chapter 12 – Review & Repeat

"Without data, you're just another person with an opinion."

- W. Edwards Deming
Engineer and Management Consultant

A number of years ago, I shattered my knee going off a ski jump. The result was that I couldn't walk for about six months. When I was able to start walking again, I had a pretty bad limp. A doctor friend of mine told me that if I ever wanted to walk again without a limp, that I needed to get on a bike and ride it every day. This actually had several benefits, besides allowing me to walk without a limp. Biking is a great exercise because there isn't the pounding on your joints like you experience with running, yet it is great for getting outside and enjoying the fresh air and sunshine. It is one of the best cardiovascular exercises there is, so it improves overall health.

Healthy people tend to be more successful in all areas of their life. This taught me that I needed to make exercise a daily part of my routine, and by doing so, I might actually accomplish more. The time you spend exercising can be used for listening to podcasts or just allowing your brain to come up with new ideas.

Here is what else I discovered. Riding a bike (or probably any form of exercise), makes you want to compete with yourself. If you have one of those little computers on your bike, it tells you how far and how fast you went. Soon you will want more data than that, and using a smart phone app live Strava Cycling allows you to keep track of how much elevation you climbed, what your average speed was for a particular ride, total miles, total time, how many calories you burned, and how you compare to others who ride the same routes you do. It also allows you to compare yourself over a period of time to see if you are improving. You can also enter in factors that the app doesn't measure, such as body weight and heart rate.

Keeping track of the above-mentioned stats makes you want to improve. If you rode your bike twenty miles one day, you will try to push yourself to ride twenty-two or twenty-five the next day. If you rode twenty miles in an hour and thirty

> *That which you measure, will improve.*

minutes, you will try to better your performance and ride that same route in an hour and twenty minutes. It turns out that if you measure something, almost anything, you will improve in those areas. It wasn't long after I started keeping track of my results before I found myself able to participate in "century rides" (100 miles), and even the "Triple Bypass," a ride through the Colorado Rockies over three mountain passes covering one hundred twenty-seven miles in a single day.

The same thing happens in business. However, many businesses fail to measure their results. Sure, they look at their sales figures and have an accountant prepare year-end financials, but they don't look at the numbers that drive those results. In the old days, marketing was difficult to quantify, but now there is no excuse. You can easily measure click-through rates, reach, cost-per-action, time spent on your site, bounce rates, total engagements, conversion rates, and of course total sales and revenues. A successful business today will look at every piece of data and try to improve on those numbers. When you do, you will find the same thing happening to your business as it did to my bike riding. You will ask yourself questions like, "How can I get one percent more conversions today than I did last week?", or "How can I get more clicks on my ad this month than I did last month?"

One characteristic of Jeff Bezos' philosophy is that he doesn't rely on intuition. Instead Amazon measures everything, then makes their decision based on facts. By making decisions based on data, he minimizes the risks Amazon takes. Everything boils down to simple math.

For your particular business, you need to define which of those metrics are the most important to you. Every business will be different, but those that are important to your business are called "key performance indicators," or KPI. Figure out what your KPI's are and then review those at a minimum of once a week, then use these strategies to repeat the sales cycle.

Your opinion doesn't count, remember? That is why you absolutely MUST review everything you are doing and determine if it is working. If it is, then great. Keep running that same ad or promotion until it is no longer is working. If it isn't, figure out how to tweak it so that it will work. Then, repeat everything you've done and keep the gears moving. That is what makes the R gear produce results.

Following are some of the ways that you can measure how well your actions are performing:

Facebook Insights
Every Facebook page owner's first stop for Facebook analytics should be their page's "Insights." This includes information about page views, page likes, reach and post engagement. In

other words, the Facebook Insights will show you how well your postings are performing with organic Facebook traffic. It does not show you your analytics from your advertisements. But by looking at these numbers you will be able to determine which posts are performing the best, and thus use those concepts when creating new posts.

Facebook Ad Analytics

You can get a lot of information from Facebook when you run an ad. Go to the Facebook Ads Manager and drill down to the ad sets you are interested in. By default, you will be shown information about each of your campaigns. Change this to view "add ads" so that you can see how each individual ad is performing. Facebook will show you link clicks, reach, and cost per click. An important number that Facebook does not show you, though it is implied in the cost per click, is the ratio of clicks per reach. It's good if you can see which ad is generating lots of clicks from the number of people the ad is displayed to. This also means that the cost per click will be lower.

The cost per click will vary depending upon what you are selling. As a general rule, if you can get this to less than fifty cents per click, you are doing well. One thing that many people overlook is the drop-down selection just above the ad analytics. This information, by default is "Performance." If you click on this, there are a number of other options you can view, including "Engagement." Often engagement is a metric that you will find useful, so be sure to look at those numbers as well. The "breakdown" pull-down will give you further information, such as age and gender of who is actually clicking on your ads. Be sure to use this information when you create your next ad set.

As I said in the chapter about advertising, it is a good idea to run multiple competing ads and compare the results of each of them. These are the tools that help you decide which one is performing the best.

AdRoll Analytics

AdRoll, of course, provides you with its own set of analytics, which while similar to Facebook, the user-interface is slightly different. When you first log in to AdRoll, the stats for your current campaigns are displayed. One of the things that AdRoll shows you, that you have to calculate yourself in Facebook, is the click-through rate (the percentage of clicks versus impressions). My personal belief is that an impression with AdRoll is worth more than an impression on Facebook, in part because the ad looks like an ad and not a boosted post. It also helps because when you are on a different site, you tend to stay on one page longer in order to read a complete article, not just short messages.

Be sure to click on the various tabs that AdRoll provides so you can get a complete picture of how your ads are performing, including the individual ads tab, segments, and placements. There is also a tab called "sites" which shows you which website your ad has appeared on.

AdSense Analytics

As we discussed earlier, AdSense is Google's program that gives the website owner the ability to place contextual ads on their site and get paid when a visitor clicks on the ad. Clearly, the objectives of AdSense analytics are different than your own ads that you placed on Facebook or AdRoll. But there are similarities, such as impressions and click-through rates. The AdSense dashboard is very graphic, so it is easy to visualize how well those ads are performing (and if you are making any money).

YouTube Analytics

YouTube has its own set of metrics. If you are creating YouTube videos, you will want to see not only how many viewed your video, but how much time they spent watching the video, and if they interacted with it.

Ecommerce Shopping Cart Analytics

Every shopping cart includes information about how many sales have been made within a specified time period. Typically, you can also get reports for sales by product and sales by category, how many times a coupon has been used, and how many visitors have viewed a certain product. You might also be able to view abandoned shopping carts. These metrics can assist you in planning your stocking requirements and future advertising campaigns.

Affiliate Analytics

Both advertisers and publishers can keep track of their efforts with the metrics provided by the affiliate program you are using. This includes clicks, unique visits, transactions, and commissions.

Influencer Review Analytics

Whether you are using influencers to help promote your products, or you are an influencer posting content for products you've reviewed, most of the review sites will provide you with a variety of statistics about your activities.

Google Analytics

One thing that you may notice, regardless of which tracking methods you are using, is that the numbers don't coincide exactly with Google Analytics. The explanation from everyone is that the discrepancy between such-and-such and Google

Analytics reports are normal due to differences in reporting methodologies. This doesn't make sense at first – after all, it seems like a visitor is a visitor and it should be easy to count. Apparently not, since everyone comes up with a different number.

Here is how AdRoll explains this (and the same principles probably apply to Facebook and other programs that track metrics): AdRoll tracks advertising clicks. However, Google Analytics tracks visits associated with your advertising. Google Analytics visits can be as short as one pageview, or last many hours and may contain multiple pageviews, events, and transactions. Visits expire after 30 minutes of inactivity. Any subsequent activity would be tracked as a separate visit.

Clicks associated with your ads may be bigger than visits because a single visitor may click your ads multiple times. When a visitor clicks multiple times within the same visit, AdRoll records multiple clicks while Google Analytics records the multiple page views as only one visit. Server latency may contribute to tracking problems and visitors may navigate away before the Google Analytics tracking code executes. Visitors may have set their preferences to opt out of Google Analytics tracking, but they may still be targeted and measured by AdRoll.

Visits associated with your ads may be bigger than clicks because a user may click on an ad, and then, during a different session, return directly to the site through a bookmark or by typing the address into the browser's location bar. In this case, the marketing attribution from the first visit is preserved, so the initial click results in more than one visit.

However, you should see similarities in trends, and that is what is most important. Are your numbers going up or are they going down? Are people staying longer on your site? Most importantly, are you getting more conversions and having your revenues go up?

Putting It All Together

We've seen how you can track and measure just about everything there is related to your digital marketing efforts. Wouldn't it be nice to keep track of everything in one place? I thought about creating a website that would do this, but there are a couple of problems:

1. Not everyone uses the same methods for their digital marketing. Everyone has a different shopping cart. Some people sell on Amazon, others on eBay. Some people use LinkShare for their affiliate programs, while others use a WordPress plugin. Everyone is different.

2. Since you usually have to log in to different channels to view your analytics, many sites won't let you embed their analytic pages into another web page. This makes it technically impossible to have a single repository of all your data in one place.

I have come up with an idea that makes it much easier for you to build your own unique dashboard with all of the solutions you use, making it easy to get to everything quickly. First head over to a site called protopage.com.

Because this isn't a technical manual, I'm not going to provide documentation on how to use this site, but rather show you how you can use it to create your own marketing dashboard. Start by opening up one of the tracking pages you wish to include on your marketing dashboard. For example, go to your Facebook Ad Manager. Create a screen capture of this page and save the image to your computer.

Now, go back to Protopage and click on "Add Widget." On the "Add a Widget" menu, choose "Photo." Browse to the screen capture image you created above, and select "Resize photo to fit inside this widget." Enter the title as "Facebook Ads" or whatever you want to call this widget. Copy the URL string from your Facebook Ads manager page and past it into the "Clickthrough URL" field. Then press "upload."

Photo upload   edit ✕

Upload a photo from your computer,
or <u>click here</u> to see a sample photo

[Browse...]   amazon-affiliates.jpg

◉ Resize photo to fit inside this widget
◯ Resize photo to fit dimensions:

[465] x [378]   pixels

Title your photo (optional)

Add a description (optional)

Clickthrough URL (optional)
iliate-program.amazon.com/home

[Upload]

Unfortunately, your dashboard will only show a static image of your results, not real-time results. Now all you have to do is click on the image to view the live results.

Repeat the above steps for each item you want to appear on your dashboard. Drag them into the order that makes the most sense for you. I like to group mine by type, such as:

Box 1: Sales Channels

- WooCommerce
- Shopify
- BigCommerce
- Magento
- ECwid

- Other

Box 2: Market Places

- Amazon
- eBay
- Overstock
- Other

Box 3: Advertising

- Facebook
- AdRoll
- Google
- Other

Box 4: Affiliates

- Amazon
- LinkShare
- JV Zoo
- Commission Junction
- Other

Box 5: Google

- Google Analytics
- Adwords
- AdSense
- YouTube

Box 6: Influencers Review Sites

- Tomoson
- Vipon
- TopInfluencer
- IZEA
- SnagShout
- Amzrc
- Other

You can also use Protopage to add a news feed URL, so that your marketing dashboard will show you all the latest posts from a particular feed. This is a great way to keep current. For example, click on "Add Widget" and enter http://webstoresltd.com/feed/ into the news feed URL. This will create a widget showing you all of my latest blog posts. You could also create another widget and enter:

https://www.youtube.com/channel/UCE74s5g7nKoLhUr6vtpTUWw

This will create a widget showing you all my latest videos on YouTube. You might want to put various pages and feeds on different tabs. Get creative. This is **your** marketing dashboard. Once you have your dashboard built, it is not set in stone. You can add to it and edit it as your needs change. Tracking your analytics is important to your marketing, and because this tool is so flexible, including providing search capabilities to the search engines of your choice, you should make this the home page you see whenever you open up your browser. This way it will be easy for you to check on your stats on a regular basis.

Chapter 13 – Research New Opportunities

"There's nothing wrong with market research as long as you remember that marketing is a game of the future. Most marketing research is a report on the past."

- Ries and Trout
Bottom-Up Marketing

As of writing this book, ecommerce, while growing faster than brick and mortar sales, still only represents 7.8 percent of all purchases. And that includes Amazon's share, which is about forty percent of total ecommerce sales. Of that eight percent, half of those online sales are made via mobile devices. You've heard lots and lots of information over the years about how important it is for you to have an ecommerce website and how you have to do mobile, and you have to show up on social media, and on and on. This is in large part due to the fact that while most purchases are made off-line, according to Hub Spot, 97% of purchasing decisions are influenced by your internet presence. But ecommerce is still in its infancy, which means that there are huge opportunities ahead, not just for large sites like Amazon, but for small merchants and startups as well. What these numbers indicate is that you have not yet missed the boat! In fact, many of these technologies are just now becoming mature enough that this is probably the best time to really make a play on the internet. If you haven't yet invested in an online sales channel, it is not too late. But you do need to get going now – JP Morgan did a study predicting that online sales will grow to fourteen percent (14%) by 2018 and perhaps thirty percent (30%) by 2020. Eddie Machaalani & Mitchell Harper, CO-CEOs of BigCommerce, claim that *"By 2022, brick and mortar retail spaces will be little more than showrooms."* Whether that is true or not, this is clearly the time to get into ecommerce.

Of course, new technologies will continue to be created. Change is inevitable. New trends in social media will continue to evolve. While it is important to continuously repeat the cycle that is making you money, you should always be on the look-out for how new technologies might affect your online business. Disruptive technologies in social commerce, mobile and customer experience have transformed the retail industry over the years, and will continue to do so. The mission for all marketers is to stay ahead of the curve and spot trends that will boost sales and provide customers with the most efficient and pleasurable online shopping experience possible. Let's discuss a few of the technologies that are likely to have an impact on your ecommerce business over the next number of years.

Google Alerts allows you to monitor the internet for interesting new content. Many people use it to see if anyone is posting information about them, and that is a great use for it. Not only can you use Google Alerts to see who is talking about you, you can keep up to date on topics that interest you. Here are some things you might want to create Google Alerts for:

Live Video

Live video was all the rage when it first came out. Facebook, in particular, helped to make this technology mainstream for everyone. Interestingly though, few businesses use it, or at least use it well. You likely are wondering what you would say. Here's my suggestion, just talk about what's new in your business. Make it conversational, just as if a customer walked into your store and asked about your latest products. Live video doesn't need to be long (in fact, you want to remain live long enough that you pick up some viewers, but not so long that you bore them). Shoot for about five minutes to start, and even when you are comfortable doing this, cut it off after about ten minutes.

Tell (and show) your viewers your latest products. Remember the video, like all marketing, should be about them, not about you. Ask questions to try to get some interaction. Acknowledge those who join you live, especially if they are interacting with you. Don't just end the video. Give them a call-to-action and a reason to watch the next time you do a live video. Just like blogging, you should probably do a minimum of one live video each week, and do it at the same time each week so that people will get used to your schedule.

360-Degree Video

Like the other technologies I discuss in this chapter, 360-degree video is not new. Years ago, I recall going to Disneyland and watching a film in the round, with a screen that completely surrounded me. When I first started developing ecommerce websites for my clients, I would set up a tripod, move the camera in about fifteen-degree increments and take a series of still photos that could then be stitched together with a bit of JavaScript code so the user could pan around and see the entire room. This same technique could be used by keeping the camera stationary, but placing an object on a turntable and moving the turntable in fifteen-degree increments instead of the camera, so you could view an object on all sides. And Google, of course, uses 360-degree cameras for their street-view mapping.

But as I am writing this, I just purchased my first 360-degree video camera. The cost has come down to where your average consumer can afford to create their own 360-degree videos or still images and share them live on Facebook or YouTube. Now anyone with a physical store can set up the camera in the middle of their store and allow virtual visitors to experience what it is like to shop in their store. Immersion videos of course are even more dramatic if there is action involved. Sports like skiing, biking, skydiving, snorkeling, or race car driving will find this technology useful. If you are a micro-influencer showing off a vendor's products, 360-degree videos can be really helpful.

One of the great things about a 360-degree video is that you can control the camera remotely using a smart phone app. Just set the camera up on a tripod in a central location, then remove yourself from the scene and use your phone to control the camera from a distance. This allows you to get shots you might not otherwise be able to get, such as animals, or even customers who might otherwise be inhibited around a camera.

Of course, these cameras shoot video, not just still images, so you can move around inside your store, giving a complete tour of the store as you walk through it. Immersive video can be done for less than two hundred dollars right now, although ultra-high definition may still run you quite a bit more. But as the costs continue to come down and the quality goes up, 360-degree video may end up being just another option on all cameras and thus become as ubiquitous as cell phones are today.

Augmented Reality

Marketers in the retail space have always faced the obstacle of getting their customers to take a leap of faith and buy their clothing and accessories online. In the past, it's been perceived as a risk for customers to buy these things online because people just like to try clothes and accessories on before committing to purchasing them. Directly addressing that barrier is virtual try-on technology, giving consumers the ability to try on clothes and accessories before making a purchase decision online--a virtual dressing room. This rising technology isn't limited to online shopping experiences. Stores like Macy's are adopting it in select locations, offering options to "try on" an outfit in every available color, find out your exact size, and offer suggestions of items to fashionably pair with your outfit.

VR Shopping

Imagine combining 360-degree videos with augmented reality to create a virtual shopping store. Your customers could essentially walk down the aisles of your store, browsing for products, then click on a product to pull it off the shelf and read the description or watch a video about the product. But you don't need a physical store with a video to do this, you could use a three-dimensional model to create this effect. Last year, Alibaba introduced virtual reality shopping for people in China to enable them to shop all over the world. This could help to improve the shopping experience, creating more engagement with your customers.

Amazon GO

Amazon describes their Amazon Go store like this: *"Amazon Go is a new kind of store with no checkout required. We created the world's most advanced shopping technology so you never have to wait in line. With our Just Walk Out Shopping experience, simply use the Amazon Go app to enter the store, take the products you want, and go! No lines, no checkout."*

The checkout-free shopping experience is made possible by using same types of technologies used in self-driving cars: computer vision, sensor fusion, and deep learning. This technology automatically detects when products are taken from or returned to the shelves and keeps track of them in a virtual cart. When you're done shopping, you can just leave the store. Shortly after, they charge your Amazon account and send you a receipt. All you need is an Amazon account, a supported smartphone, and the free Amazon Go app.

Currently there is only one Amazon Go store, located in Seattle, Washington, and it is still in beta testing. But once again, this technology could totally disrupt retail sales as we know them today. Sure, you would still need stockers, but combined with facial recognition advertising which I discuss later, the need for sales clerks and checkout staff are eliminated.

The Internet of Things

The "Internet of Things" (IoT) is becoming an increasingly growing topic of conversation. The concept is basically that anything with an on/off switch can be connected to the internet and to each other. This not only includes cellphones, but appliances, lights, wearable devices, and even clothes. This also applies to components of machines. For example, a jet engine of an airplane or the drill of an oil rig will be able to connect. The new rule for the future is going to be, "Anything that can be connected, will be connected." The analyst firm Gartner says that by 2020 there will be over 26 billion connected devices.

But why on earth would you want so many connected devices talking to each other? One example might be that you are on your way to a meeting, your car could have access to your calendar and already know the best route to take. If the traffic is heavy, your car might send a text to the other party notifying them that you will be late. Perhaps your alarm clock wakes up you at 6 a.m. and then notifies your coffee maker to start brewing coffee for you. Or your office equipment knew when it was running low on supplies and automatically re-ordered more.

Clearly these types of automated connections will have an enormous impact on ecommerce and our daily lives. But it will also bring about a new set of challenges, especially as it relates to security.

Artificial Intelligence

A number of companies already employ artificial intelligence or AI in their ecommerce processes today. For example, Netflix uses AI to provide personalized recommendations to subscribers based on their previous streaming habits. Personalization, of course, is only one aspect of AI. AI gives computer systems the ability to perform tasks that normally require human intelligence such as how a shopper buys things. This may include visual perception, speech recognition, decision-making, translation between languages, visual searches and virtual personal shoppers.

Many aspects of AI have made significant strides in the past few years, especially voice recognition. Asking a machine to do a certain task is no longer science fiction. This does not mean that machines now have the ability to reason, but they certainly can make shopping recommendations.

Facial Recognition Advertising

You may remember seeing Tom Cruise in *Minority Report* being recognized and served intrusive, personalized advertising as he tries to escape a futuristic city. That is facial recognition advertising and it is here to stay. Consumers walking past billboards can now see and hear real-time, personalized marketing based on their genders, ages and even moods.

Consumers are already concerned about privacy, but can you imagine when facial recognition advertising identifies you as an individual and calls you by name, as you walk by a monitor in WalMart? The technology probably won't be limited to physical stores, as most devices are already equipped with a camera, even if you aren't logged into a specific website, you could be recognized and targeted based upon past shopping trends.

Biometric authentication

The technology making the biggest difference to payment completion today is biometrics, largely thanks to the proliferation of fingerprint readers in smartphones. Both Apple Pay and Samsung Pay use biometric authentication today, and as this technology becomes more sophisticated, it will become more widely adapted.

Federated identity

Federated identity management (FIM) is an arrangement that can be made among multiple enterprises that allows subscribers to use the same identification data to obtain access to the networks of all enterprises in the group. The ultimate goal of identity federation is to enable users of one domain to securely access data or systems of another domain seamlessly, and without the need for completely redundant user administration. Facebook, Google and LinkedIn are the leaders in federated identity but banks, telecom companies, and governments will soon enter the space as well. Does your ecommerce site currently allow customers to "Log in with Facebook", thus eliminating the need to re-enter their user information? Customers may soon expect this during the checkout process.

Tokenization

Tokenization is a super-buzzy payments word at the moment, especially because of the increased attention on mobile payments apps like Apple Pay. Basically, tokenization adds an extra level of security to sensitive credit card data. Tokenization is the process of protecting sensitive data by replacing it with an algorithmically generated number called a token. Often times tokenization is used to prevent credit card fraud. In credit card tokenization, the customer's primary account number (PAN) is replaced with a series of randomly-generated numbers, which is called the token. Just like the nationwide shift to chip cards, tokenization's end game is to prevent the bad guys from duplicating your bank information onto another card. But while chip cards protect against fraud that occurs when someone pays at a physical store, tokenization is primarily designed to fight online or digital breaches. Employing tokenization won't in and of itself make you PCI compliant, but it's considered a "best practice." When you use a payment system such as Stripe, Square, or other payment aggregators, these systems are already employing tokenization, so you don't have to worry about the technicalities. What this does point out, however, is that online payment methods will continue to evolve and it is a good idea to remain knowledgeable about how this affects your ecommerce business.

Near Field Communication (NFC)

Everything in this chapter, of course, has to do with the future of technology and how it affects ecommerce. In addition to these items, there are specific items related to your niche. Regardless of what business you are in, you will want to keep up with what is happening in your industry. In an ever-changing market and world, it's more important than ever to stay current, competitive and up-to-date. Take the time to become a life-long student.

3D Printing

It has been a few years since I've been involved in the CAD or Computer aided design Industry, but a few years ago I visited Autodesk. While there, I was taken on a tour of their design gallery and shown a 3D printer. I am usually asked to speak about ecommerce and selling products on the internet. So, what is a 3D printer and what does it have to do with ecommerce? Perhaps a lot, as I'll soon discuss.

Since 2003 there has been large growth in the sale of 3D printers. I've seen shows and videos about 3D printing technology before, but had never seen an actual object printed in 3D. A primary difference between 3D printing and traditional CAD/CAM technologies is that it is an additive process rather than a subtractive process. Size is not an issue. While at Autodesk, I saw printed parts that required a microscope to reveal the workings of a watch sitting next to a full-size motorcycle that had been printed in 3D. Even an entire car, the Urbee, has been printed in 3D.

3D printers can be used to create virtually any object directly from a computer-aided-design. The technology has been described as a machine that can turn a blueprint into a physical object. Feed it a design for a wrench, and it produces a physical, working wrench. Scan a coffee mug with a 3D scanner and sending the file to the printer can produce thousands of identical mugs.

Even today there are a number of competing designs for 3D printers, most work in the same general way. Instead of taking a block of material and cutting away until it produces an object, a 3D printer actually builds the object up from tiny bits of material, layer by layer. Among other advantages, a 3D printer can create structures that would be impossible to make because the designer would need to find a way to insert a cutting tool into a solid block of material.

Because they create objects by building them up layer-by-layer, 3D printers can create objects with internal, movable parts. Instead of having to print individual parts and have a person assemble them, a 3D printer can print the object already assembled. Of course, a 3D printer can also print individual parts or replacement parts. In fact, some 3D printers can print a substantial number of their own parts, essentially allowing them to self-replicate.

Because of my involvement in the green industry and my background with using AutoCAD for landscape design, I was joking with the Autodesk employees about being able to print a flower or shrub in 3D. No, this isn't possible yet, but you can print with a variety of materials, including plastic, ceramics, glass and metal. Wouldn't it be great if the "ink" or raw materials for 3D printing could come from waste packaging or recyclable material like plastic from bottles that most of us have in our homes?

3D printing technology is currently being studied by biotechnology firms and academia for possible use in tissue engineering applications where organs and body parts are built using 3D printing techniques. Layers of living cells are deposited onto a gel medium and slowly built up to form three dimensional structures. 3D printing can produce a personalized hip replacement in one pass, with the ball permanently inside the socket, and even at current printing resolutions, the unit will not require polishing. The first human vein has already been created with 3D printing. If that is possible, printing a plant in 3D may just become reality.

So back to the question, what does all this have to do with ecommerce? We are already accustomed to many digital downloadable products from music to books. Certainly, a manufacturer could create made to order products with this technology. What if the price of a 3D printer drops to where they become as common as 2D printers? You would simply download a design, then print the product yourself! Imagine going to an online store and using a visualization program, the store can show you what a pair of shoes will look like on your feet. If you like what you see, you download the 3D file, specify your shoe size and desired color, and print out the shoes to wear that very evening.

The technology exists for us to do this today! In fact, Continuum Fashion and Shapeways have already launched the world's first fully 3D-printed bikini. The N12 bikini is named after nylon 12, a strong yet flexible material that can be printed as thin as 0.7 millimeters without breaking. It's also waterproof, with a texture said to resemble seashell when wet. The bikini comprises circular plates, each varying in size based on the curvature of the would-be wearer's form.

Did you ever see any of the Star Trek episodes where they used a device called a replicator to produce a cup of hot tea? The personal communication device or flip phone was created as a result of the imagination of Star Trek, and it appears that a replicator is not far behind.

We are at the early stages of this technology. The Makerbot is akin to what the Apple I was back in the early days of the personal computer. It is basically a kit for technology hobbyists, while commercial 3D printers and the raw materials for printing are expensive, not unlike a mainframe computer. But it is starting to happen. A prosthetic leg typically costs about $60,000. A 3D-printed leg that is more realistic and has more features can be made for about $6,000. Cost savings are already a benefit in this industry.

A California start-up is even working on building houses. Its printer, which would fit on a tractor-trailer, would use patterns delivered by computer, squirt out layers of special concrete and build entire walls that could be connected to form the basis of a house. It is manufacturing with a mouse click instead of hammers, nails and workers. Advocates of the technology say that by doing away with manual labor, 3D printing could revamp the economics of manufacturing and revive American industry as creativity and ingenuity replace labor costs as the main concern around a variety of goods. In other words, we could eliminate our dependency on China for manufactured products.

But today, piracy affects film, TV, games, apps, news and other digital files as people share everything. We all know what happened in the entertainment industry. It was easy to copy files and, as a result we did just that. What if you have a copyrighted design that is suddenly shared on the internet? It is impossible to foresee the long-term impact of 3D printing. But the technology is coming, and it is likely to disrupt every field it touches.

An evolution of our economy is about to dawn. Everything that is made by any company in the world can be stolen, uploaded and shared for people to print at home. Our entire economy as we know it may be at its end. Something new is about to happen, and we get to live during this time of change.

S: The Sun Gear - Strategy

"Without strategy, execution is aimless. Without execution, strategy is useless."

- Morris Chang
CEO of TSMC

FOREWORD by Ken McArthur

By this stage, you should be starting to create your own personal action plan. You can start as simply as sketching out a flow chart of what you want to do on a piece of paper. This will become your strategy or the focal point of your business. Strategy is NOT goal setting. Strategy is about HOW you are going to accomplish the **actions** of your guiding principles.

If you are like me, you don't just want to have a business to make money, but you want to create an impact. You want to provide meaning and purpose in the lives of your customers.

The best way that I know to have impact is to focus on key actions that directly impact the core elements of a process. There's no word in the English language for what I want to express so I've made one up.

Let's call that impact the "coreaction factor" and say that "coreactions" are actions that have the most impact on any result. In any process, there are key pivot points or "coreactions" where choosing a particular direction will change the outcome exponentially and persistently. Typically, "coreactions" are passionate, permanent, and prevalent. In this section of his book, Greg calls this "obsession."

I've made it my mission to crack the "Impact Factor" by identifying the actions that impact your bottom-line most. We all know that businesses sell something (products services, etc.) and in business we want to sell at a profit. If we can find a product or service that makes a profit, then:

Product or Service + Sales + Profit = A Business

Not necessarily a seven-figure one, but still a business. You must do the math and determine how many units you need to sell at what price and calculate the tradeoff of time versus future profits. You need to build up a list of customers. You then add value for those customers. You must factor in customer support.

So now you have your strategic plan. You are obsessed with creating an impact through your business. But there is one more thing. You have to take action. That's the hard part. Greg calls this "execution."

By taking action, or executing your plan, you will achieve more than ninety-nine percent of those who start a business. Along the way, you will discover that you can't do it all by yourself. You must get others to help. By working together, we can do so much more than we can alone.

If you want to have impact right now and reach millions with your ideas, products and services, then you must follow each of these steps. Create a strategic action plan. Be obsessed. Get others to join your cause. Then execute. Bottom-line, there IS a way to make magic and the choice is up to YOU!

Ken McArthur
Movie producer, best-selling author, entrepreneur, marketer, event producer
The Impact Factor
http://kenmcarthur.com/

Chapter 14 – Strategy, Execution & Obsession

"Strategy is simply resource allocation. When you strip away all the noise, that's what it comes down to. Strategy means making clear cut choices about how to compete. You cannot be everything to everybody, no matter what the size of your business or how deep its pockets."

- Jack Welch
CEO General Electric

Why is it that Bill Gates and Steve Jobs achieved more success than many other equally, or more, talented computer geeks (myself included?) Why is it that some people can eat certain foods and do a certain level of exercise, yet they can never compete with someone else who is doing the exact same thing? And why is it that one individual can perform certain activities and copy them exactly as someone else, and never achieve the same level of success in business as the person they are copying? I've asked myself these questions many times. I have had more failures than successes in my business career, and even when I do the exact same things as others, I have never reached the same level of success as some of my peers. Are they smarter than me? Do they know something I don't?

As I've pondered these questions, I realize that there are three key components that make any system work. I've given you a system in this book, and I've seen it work for some of my clients, yet not work for others, even when they are in the same niche, and perhaps in the same town. Two companies may follow the mechanics of the system, yet one succeeds and the other fails. The reasons usually come down to these factors:

- Strategy
- Execution
- Obsession

Perhaps this is what SEO should really stand for. I started this book by questioning the traditional marketing funnel and now I'm redefining SEO. Many internet marketers may see me as a heretic, but hear me out.

Strategy, execution and obsession is the core of the GEARS system. The central sun gear should really be the starting point for your online success. Everything revolves around the sun gear, just as everything in your business should revolve around your strategy, execution, and obsession.

Strategy

This book has discussed various ways to connect with your customers through content marketing, especially using others, such as your customers and industry-specific micro-influencers, to generate that content for you. Yet few companies today have a strategy in place that allows them to generate content in an on-going and meaningful way. Even fewer have a strategy to engage with influencers. You can't just hire an influencer and expect results. You can only create massive results by having a clearly defined strategy revolving around goals, metrics of success, content, and relationship management.

When developing a strategy to use with influencers, follow these steps:

- Set a goal
- Determine your metrics of success
- Determine how you want to work with influencers based on your goals
- Define your method of compensation
- Create a list of influencers who will help you reach your goal
- Develop your pitch
- Conduct the outreach
- Follow up & negotiate
- Share influencer's content/engage with them
- Thank the influencer and ask if they are open to other opportunities
- Measure success of the campaign
- Continue engaging with the influencer to keep the relationship going

Amazon's mission is to have the most customer-centric website in the world. Their strategy to accomplish this includes many of the methods I've described in this book, including using affiliates, getting quality product reviews, utilizing retargeting ads, continuous automated emails as follow up, measuring and monitoring everything about their business to see how they can improve, and even a public email address for Jeff Bezos, the CEO.

Execution

Strategy is good, even essential, but until you act on your strategy it is just an idea. And ideas by themselves are worthless. The marketplace rewards execution, not ideas. If Apple had only thought of a smart phone, but not delivered, the iPhone would never have become the best-selling product of all time. The iPhone is not only the best-selling mobile phone but also the best-selling music player, the best-selling camera, the best-selling video screen and the best-selling computer of all time. It is, quite simply, the best-selling product of all time. And the reason was execution.

A great example of execution is the story of Chad Pregracke. Chad grew up in East Moline, Illinois, where the Mississippi River was in his backyard. As a teenager, he worked as a commercial shell diver and began to notice the heaps of debris in the fabled waterway. This river supplies drinking water to 18 million people in more than 50 U.S. cities. Tires, appliances, old cars, tractors, and tons of litter were dumped into the river. "I got sick of seeing it and just wanted to do something about it," he said.

At the age of 17, he started making calls to government agencies to notify them of the problem, assuming someone would take care of it. Year after year passed by and the problem only worsened. In 1997, Chad decided that if no one else was going to clean up the river, he would.

"I just saw all this trash on the islands. Nobody was picking it up. So, I did," he says.

After filling his flat-bottomed boat several times over with old tires, oil drums, appliances and junk of all kinds, he unloaded it onto the dock at his parents' house to be sorted and recycled. His folks, "weren't too thrilled with that," he says.

When just 23, he landed his first corporate sponsor. "I was walking past the TV at a buddy's house and saw this NASCAR driver get out of his car, and he had all these corporate logos all over his suit. I said to myself, 'That's what I need, logos.'" More specifically, the corporate money behind the logos. Of course, he had no idea how to get sponsors, so he looked in the phone book and started with the A's. Alcoa was first on his list.

Tim Wilkinson was a vice president of Alcoa at the time, and didn't take unsolicited calls, but Chad didn't know that. He walked in and talked to the secretary. Wilkinson recalls, "The receptionist walked back to my office and said there's a young man in bib overalls and a baseball cap with long hair who wants to talk to you about cleaning up the Mississippi River."

Intrigued and inspired by Pregracke's "unbridled enthusiasm" and dedication to his vision, Wilkinson held open the door to eventual funding, provided Chad would bring back a plan and a budget.

"I said, 'No problem,' but I didn't have a clue how to form a business plan or make up a budget," says Pregracke. He enlisted the help of his mom and eventually got funded for $8,400. He spent that summer cleaning a 35-mile stretch of the river by himself. By year's end, he had single-handedly pulled around 45,000 pounds of trash out of the river.

Just as Pregracke was inspired by NASCAR logos to ask for corporate help, maneuvering his small boat around the massive grain barges moving up and down the river led him to the conclusion, "I need a barge." Ingram Barge Co., which runs 1,000 barges on the Mississippi, Ohio and Illinois rivers, became an early corporate sponsor.

To date, about 70,000 volunteers have joined his crusade, helping him collect more than 7 million pounds of debris through his nonprofit, Living Lands & Waters. "As far as trash and garbage goes, I've seen what I like to call social change happen on the upper Mississippi River, as well as the Illinois River," Chad says. "People are not treating the river as bad as they once were. It's hard to find a pop can in some places."

But here is the thing: Chad Pregracke was very much a micro-influencer. He was just one guy when he started. But unlike so many others, he acted upon what he felt needed to be done. He executed his plan. And his results were massive.

Obsession

I talked about how Amazon's strategy was to be the world's most customer-centric website, but for Jeff Bezos, this is more than just a strategy, it's an obsession. Bezos has said, "The most important single thing is to focus obsessively on the customer. Our goal is to be earth's most customer-centric company." And yet another time, "If you're truly obsessed about your customers" Bezos says, "it will cover a lot of your other mistakes." Obsession over customers is ingrained into the company culture and permeates everything Amazon does.

Whether you call it obsession, a passion for what you are doing, fanatical, or intensity on how you execute your strategy, this singular focus is what will set you apart from your competition. It's not your unique selling proposition (USP) that makes you unique, it's your unwavering focus and determination that will set you apart from everyone else.

Grant Cardone, motivational speaker and author, says, "Obsession is the fuel that gives you a can't-quit, won't-quit, accelerator-to-the-floor monster ambition inside of you and it grows as you grow regardless of your age. In fact, the older I get and the more success I experience, the more obsessed I become with the reality I can create. As you embrace your obsessions and deny average, your potential will continue to be revealed to you. This is what keeps people motivated and creating. It is not money or awards but possibilities. Becoming satisfied with what you have done only means someone in your life has convinced you to settle for average."

Simon Jackson was far from being an average kid. Like Chad Pregracke in the previous story, Simon was a micro-influencer with a mission. His passion for bears started when he was seven years old and saw a bear on a family camping trip. "I came to realize that humans had an option. We had the power to destroy or preserve these magnificent monarchs of the wilderness," said Simon. He set up a lemonade stand in grade two and raised $60 to protect grizzly bears. A few years later, Simon heard about the endangered Kermode bears and set out on a mission to protect them. "Many people ask me why I chose to campaign for the future of the Spirit bear rather than other endangered animals such as the panda or the elephant," Simon explains. "As I saw it, the Spirit bear was as unique to the world as the panda bear is to China and lived only in my home province of British Columbia. This bear, I thought, deserved our admiration, respect and most of all, our protection. I knew I had to help."

At the age of 13, Simon started the Spirit Bear Youth Coalition (SBYC). That was in 1995. Armed with a slide projector and a bus pass he began to visit high schools in British Columbia to raise awareness among his peers about his campaign and to give them a chance to get involved. Jackson didn't just have a strategic plan, he was obsessed! He persuaded 700 kids to write letters asking the government to keep logging companies out of the bear's habitat. In 1996, the BC government received more letters about the Kermode bear than any other preservation issue!

With the help and support of around six million SBYC members around the world, including naturalist Jane Goodall, and celebrities like Charlotte Church and Kevin Richardson of the Backstreet Boys, two thirds of the bear's habitat are now legally protected. That is a massive result from a single micro-influencer.

If you implement the methods I've described here today and you are totally obsessed about one thing, you will overcome the 80 to 97% who haven't figured it out. As Thomas Aquinas said, *"I fear the man of a single idea."*

Conclusion

"It is not the strongest of the species that survives, nor the most intelligent, but the one most responsive to change."

- Charles Darwin, 1809

Do you remember Blockbuster or Redbox? As online video streaming gained momentum, those companies didn't change with the times. What about Kodak, Borders Bookstores, or Blackberry? Eventually every company must change or cease to exist. Some have done a good job of this over the years. For example, Dupont, John Deere and Procter and Gamble are some of America's oldest companies. I mentioned at the beginning of this book how I had to transition from doing website design to offering internet marketing and consulting services. You must adapt if you want to remain relevant for the long haul.

Of course, adapting new technologies can be risky if they go in the other direction as well. Early adaptors often find that they spend too much time and money on a new trend and also don't make it over the long haul. A recent example is Blab – a great concept for live video and decent implementation, but they didn't make it. It might be an issue of scale or of the community it served, but ultimately, I believe it was because they didn't define what problem they were trying to solve. If you aren't solving a problem that no one else is solving, you become a commodity. Those with the deepest pockets are the ones that win the commodity game. When you are solving a specific problem for a specific group of people, you can become a market leader. You provide value that no one else is providing.

Market leaders, even a very small niche market, such as scouting certificates or landscape design software, tend to get there by having a group of enthusiastic evangelists promoting their products or services. Those influencers are the ones you want to cultivate.

You, no doubt, have heard the saying, "it's not what you know, it's who you know." In fact, it isn't who you know, it's who knows you. This book has provided several examples of this, from using Thunderclap.it to the discussion on borrowing influence. The reason why influencer marketing is so powerful is not because a particular influencer has a large following, but because the people who know that influencer believe what he or she has to say is valuable. Even with a small following, you have an impact on the world.

My friend and colleague Ken McArthur likes to say, "We all impact people, whether we want to or not." I thought about this as I was on a recent trip to Arizona. Back when I was in graduate school I worked for a landscape architecture firm where we had a project to design a new freeway system in Phoenix. At the time, all of the intersections were pretty boring. Most just had a bunch of gravel in them with a few cactus and shrubs. I came up with this idea that we should draw upon the history of the area and include Native American graphics in these areas, using different colors and textures of rock as well as the concrete to create murals that people could enjoy as they drove by. Now, most of the highways around the area incorporate this idea into the landscape design. I was a micro-influencer and didn't even know it.

Micro-influencers are all around us, and we may not even be aware of it. Think peer-pressure or social proof. I remember traveling to Dallas recently with my wife and we were looking for a place to eat. We drove by this one restaurant that had lots of cars outside. My wife said, "That's where I want to go!" Simply based on the fact that lots of other people were eating there, she assumed it must be good. We all do this, remember when your parents asked you, "Just because all your friends are jumping off a bridge, would you do it?" The answer is probably, YES! You have been influenced by others. This happens in marketing all the time.

If you have more than one person providing that influence, you are even more likely to follow the crowd. This builds momentum and it is what businesses strive to achieve. Whether you are a company looking for others to generate content and share it with their followers, or you are an expert who is sharing knowledge for something you are passionate about, influencer marketing is here to stay. You simply need to recognize that multiple micro-influencers can actually produce bigger outcomes than a single macro-influencer. The results can be massive.

None of the ideas presented in this book have been unique to me. They are the same methods used by every successful online business. I have arranged them around the GEARS acronym to make it easy to understand and remember the core concepts. What it all boils down to is having a strategy and mission and creating authentic content around that strategy. Content connects you with your customers in better ways. It builds relationships. Instead of pitching products or services, you are delivering information that makes your customer more intelligent. This is true whether you are blogging, sending out email newsletters, posting on social media, writing advertising content, creating videos, writing copy about what you offer, or providing free content in exchange for contact information.

You really need to do it all. Show up everywhere and anywhere that your prospects might be hanging out online. They won't be able to miss you, and that is essential in today's marketing. If you are starting to feel like a publisher of content instead of just a provider of products and services, you are doing it right! Now you are becoming a trusted expert that is a resource for your customers. You are one of the micro-influencers that can create massive results.

This formula works for companies as well as individuals, but with a slight twist. Rather than being the one to create reviews and receive product, you are the one setting up affiliate programs, giving away product for reviews, and creating the retargeted ads for people to display on their websites. If you are serious about gearing up your online sales, you must use multiple gears, not just one or two. Charles Shultz said, *"Life is like a 10-speed bicycle, most of us have gears we never use."* Don't be selective with the methods I've described here today, use them all. When you do, your business will run like a well-oiled machine.

I'm going to leave you with one final example. I recently went to an event about LinkedIn. The "bait" that the organizer used to draw people in was a free LinkedIn profile photo. If you came, they would give you a free headshot taken by a professional photographer (you could in fact use this photo however you wanted, but since the seminar was about LinkedIn, the tie in to having it be your LinkedIn headshot worked great). The seminar was held at a Microsoft store. It was not a Microsoft seminar, rather it was an independent group. The fact that it was held at a Microsoft store, however, implied an endorsement and certainly created influence with the audience. As a result, people attended and shared their experience with others. You too can get creative and use the GEARS system in your organization, for both products and services.

I've presented you with lots of ideas in this book. Your mind might very well be wondering, "how can I possibly keep up with all this?" Just writing a weekly blog, posting on Facebook, and creating digital ads has me overwhelmed already! That is where I can help you. For over two decades I have helped businesses stay on top of digital marketing and ecommerce.

At the beginning of this book, I talked about a formula of multiplying a random number times the current time to generate unique results. As I look back on my years in business and helping others with their businesses, I realized that if I multiply all the seemingly random events in my life, times the amount of time I've put into learning what I've taught you in this book, I can generate unique results for my clients as well.

I'd love to speak to your organization and/or consult with your business on the challenges you face with your online marketing and digital advertising. Drop me a line at

greg@gregjameson.com

or call me toll-free at 877-924-1414.

Epilogue

"I would NEVER do that!" That is the reaction that most people give you when you tell them you are going to jump out of an airplane. Inside they are thinking, "Are you crazy?"

Several years ago, I was at an internet marketing conference called JV Alert (It was later renamed to The Impact Event). While I was there I met a guy, who became a good friend of mine, named Chasen.

Chasen and I were skiing together this past spring and started talking about skydiving. He told me he was taking his daughters skydiving because he wanted them to learn that if you could conquer your fears of jumping out of an airplane, there was nothing you couldn't do.

Fast forward to my 60th birthday this year: My kids decided that for my birthday, it would be a good idea for me to go skydiving. Seriously? Why would I want to do that? Never-the-less, I played along, and before I knew it, they had purchased a skydiving package. Talk about the influencer effect!

Here's the problem: I had way too much time to think about this. I got the "gift" 2 weeks before my birthday, but my wife wanted me to wait until after I had actually turned 60 (you know, just in case...). So, we scheduled the jump for the weekend after I turned 60. Due to scheduling conflicts, we couldn't go that weekend. Good, I was off the hook! (at least for now). We scheduled it for the following weekend – but then

219

it snowed. In fact, it snowed a foot! So, we certainly couldn't go then. It got pushed out another week.

This last Saturday it was clear and sunny. In fact, it was 80 degrees and no wind. Now what? My son's friend who is in the Air Force and has done over 100 jumps came over to our house and was telling me what to expect. "Should I wear hiking boots?" I asked, thinking that I wanted to protect me ankles. No, wear old heavy jeans – you will land on your keister.

I couldn't sleep the night before – I kept waking up wondering what I was doing. Yeah, I was nervous. Heck, I was scared!

We got up the next morning to drive to the airfield. The jump site was an hour and half from our house. When we got there, there was more waiting. We were told to watch this video, which was narrated by the guy who invented tandem parachute jumping in the 1980's. Basically he spent 10 minutes telling us how everything about parachute jumping was not only dangerous, but that you would likely die. The plane could fail. The parachute could fail. The harness could fail. The instructor could fail. You could fail! Then we were handed a form that we had to sign saying that we understood that the sky diving company was not liable for any reason whatsoever. In fact, they weren't even insured! If anything went wrong, you could not sue. You had to disclose all medical conditions and sign your life away.

Now get on the scale, we want to weigh you! The scale was clearly 10 pounds heavy as I had just weighed myself that morning, but this was one time that I didn't argue. In fact, I was like, "Can you add a few more pounds to that, just to make sure that the parachute is big enough?"

We waited a little longer for the instructor to arrive. My wife struck up a conversation with the guy who was jumping after we were. "I love this part of Colorado - it is one of the prettiest parts of the state, don't you agree?" "Yeah, I spent the last 30 years here in the maximum-security prison. It is good to see what it looks like from the outside!" Clearly this guy was determined to take advantage of the rest of his life, experiencing it all now that he wasn't confined to a cell. I wondered, how many of us are confined to cells of our own making, and not experiencing life it its fullest? I thought about one of my past employees, who ended up being paralyzed from the waist down – she too had jumped out of an airplane – after she was paralyzed. She wasn't letting her condition preventing her from living her life to the fullest. And ultimately, I think that is why people jump out of airplanes – yes, it is to overcome fear, but more importantly, to really live life.

My wife turned to one of the instructors, "How long have you been doing this? I want to make sure my husband and son are going with someone experienced." The instructor replied, "I've lost count after 2000 jumps. But the guy flying with your husband is the one who taught me and he has over 10,000 jumps." OK, maybe I felt a little better. One of the other students asked, "How come you guys wear helmets and we don't?" Honestly, I was wondering the same thing. He said it was because when the parachute came out, it might hit them in the head, and we were being shielded by them, so we didn't need one. Also, they had a full-face mask to protect themselves in case the student decided to vomit. Gee – thanks!

We watched the previous jumpers land at the designated landing spot. That looked easy enough! I was ready!

We boarded the plane, if that is what you want to call it. This plane was really a single person plane with a small cargo area in it. We crammed four large adults into that tin can. It was extremely cramped and claustrophobic. I could barely squeeze in and wasn't sure how I would get out. Maybe this was their way of making sure you wanted to get out!

We took off down the run way and soon lifted into the air. We climbed until we were well over 14,000 feet. The view was incredible. From where we were, you could see almost every 14,000-foot peak in Colorado. To the south were the Sangre de Cristo's, to the west the Collegiate range, and to the north, Pike's Peak. To the east was the Pueblo Reservoir, and directly below us was the Royal Gorge. I thought back to my white-water rafting experience on the Arkansas River below us, running class 5 rapids and the instructor telling us that we didn't need helmets. We ended up doing the white-water swim for over half a mile as the water and rocks raged around us. I tried to remain calm, almost in a Zen-like meditation state as I said a few prayers.

"OK, it's time!", said my instructor as he opened the door of the plane. Now I have to tell you that being in a plane with an open door is not a natural feeling. He put his foot on this little step that was about 16" x 16" inches and told me to do the same. I couldn't bend my knees enough to obey! I struggled and tried to force my legs out – finally the other instructor grabbed my legs and pushed! I was standing on this little platform, 14,000 feet in the air, and looked at the tail of the plane, just a few feet away. "Don't worry, you won't hit anything – you're going to drop like a rock!" yelled my instructor. "Go ahead and yell – God wants to know that you are alive!" In fact, like the ex-con waiting down below, or my paralyzed friend, I knew that God really wanted us to feel as if we were truly living, and this was certainly one of those moments. "On three, we'll go – One Two" – AHHHH! He didn't wait until three as they don't want you to grab anything. We did a front flip out of the plane and started plummeting toward the earth at 140 miles per hour! I looked up and saw the plane flying away. Then – silence. Total silence. The only other time in my life that I had not heard a sound at all was when I slept in a snow cave and everything was cancelled out.

At that moment, you experience complete bliss and tranquility. You have no reference as to how fast you are falling, so you aren't aware of speed. You just put your arms out and fly.

Some 20 to 30 seconds later, the instructor opens the parachute and you are jerked back to reality. He hands you the controls and you get to fly this thing by yourself – going wherever you want until it is time to land. The accuracy of a parachute today is amazing – we landed exactly where we were supposed to, although we hit pretty hard. I learned later that our chute had a malfunction that didn't allow it to flare as much as it should have as we touched down, causing us to hit harder than expected. But I was excited! I had actually done this thing! I had conquered my fears and proven to myself that I could do anything. If you think public speaking will help you overcome your fears, try jumping out of an airplane!

My friend Chasen was right. There is nothing that you can't do. Look, whether you ever decide to jump out of an airplane or not doesn't matter. What matters is that you realize that you have a potential in you that will only be realized when you let go of your fears and understand that you can do anything you put your mind to.

I hope I've influenced you to go live your dreams.

Appendix

Checklist of 80 Actions You Can Take

G – Generate Interest

Give something Away

1. Make a list of at least ten items that you might be able to give away.

2. Invite others to review your give-away.

3. Create a test for each item to see which one gives you the best results.

4. Build a landing page to capture emails with your free product.

Get Upsells

5. Figure out what you can sell that goes with your free product.

6. Research suppliers for possible upsells.

7. Test multiple upsells to see which ones generate the most sales.

Give them a reason to come back

8. Write a new blog post.

9. Change the lead story on your home page.

10. Create a new offer for followers to check out.

11. Do a Facebook Live video.

12. Make a new YouTube video.

13. Create a survey.

14. Create a new landing page.

15. Take new photos of your products.

16. Write new product descriptions.

17. Ask customers to leave a product review.

E – Empower Influencers

Endorsements & Reviews

18. Sign up with an influencer site like Tomoson.

19. Create a give-away t-shirt.

20. Hold a contest asking people to post selfies while wearing your t-shirt.

21. Find a product to review and purchase it.

22. Take a photo of you using the product.

23. Write a product review for the purchased product and post to the website where you purchased it.

24. Create a product review video and post it to YouTube. Include your affiliate link where someone can buy it.

25. Write a blog post that includes your product review.

26. Tweet about your blog post with a link to it.

27. Post your product review photo on Instagram.

28. Post Your product review photo to Pinterest.

29. Let the company, whose product you reviewed, know about it and send them the links to your reviews.

30. Start a podcast or video cast.

31. Invite a celebrity to be a special guest that you interview on your podcast.

Engage Affiliates

32. Sign up with an affiliate site like LinkShare.

33. Create an email with your affiliate link to a product.

34. Create a YouTube video with an affiliate link to a product.

35. Create affiliate ads for your products that others can use.

36. Place an affiliate ad for a product you believe in on your website.

Earn Even More!

37. Create a buyer persona for your products.

38. Write copy for your products as if you are talking directly to your buyer persona.

39. Photograph your products being used. Use these images instead of still product shots.

40. Sign up for an eBay account.

41. Sell your excess inventory on eBay or Overstock.

42. List excess inventory on Craig's List.

43. Give away a product to one of your customers.

Amplify Your Message

Advertise

44. Sign up for an AdSense Account.

45. Create a Facebook "Boosted Post".

46. Create three Facebook Newsfeed Ads and run them for 48 hours.

47. Create landing pages for the ads so you can drive your traffic there.

48. Add the Facebook pixel to your landing page.

49. Check on your Facebook ads to see which one is performing the best. Turn off the lowest performers.

50. Sign up for an AdRoll account.

51.Add your AdRoll tracking pixel to your landing pages.

52. Create banner ads to upload to AdRoll that use the same concept as your winning Facebook ad.

Automatic Emails

53. Install MailPoet or similar software.

54. Create a newsletter template.

55. Install Microblog Poster or similar software.

56. Collect email addresses from every customer that walks in your store.

57. Import your existing email contacts into your list.

58. Segment your email list into multiple categories.

59. Write a blog post that becomes the lead story for your email newsletter.

Attend Live Events

60. Join a MeetUp group (and go to a meeting!)

61. Go to a trade show as an attendee.

62. Exhibit at a trade show.

63. Volunteer.

Results

Revenue

64. Sign up for a PayPal account.

65. Sign up for a Stripe account.

66. Add a shopping cart system like WooCommerce to your site.

67. Get an SSL certificate for your site.

Review & Repeat

68. Sign up for a Google analytics account.

69. Login to your Google analytics account and review the numbers.

70. Make changes to your plan to improve your bounce rate.

71. Adjust your plan to increase visitors.

72. Adjust your plan to improve conversions.

Research New Opportunities

73. Subscribe to an RSS feed in your industry.

74. Read at least one article per day about the trends in your market.

75. Actively seek out a demo (either at a tradeshow or online) of a new piece of technology related to your industry.

Strategy

76. Write down your Unique Selling Proposition (USP) in one sentence.

77. What is your strategy for implementing that USP?

78. How are you executing your strategy each and every day?

79. Can your customers tell others what your mission is?

80. How are you showing your customers that you are obsessed with achieving that mission?

About the Author

Greg Jameson has been at the forefront of digital commerce since the start and brings 30+ years of web development and e-commerce mastery. Greg has a history of bringing the technical, leadership, and communication skills to large organizations like Chase Paymentech, Ball Aerospace and Los Alamos Labs. As the President of WebStores Ltd., he is now focusing this expertise on businesses that need a profitable web presence.

Greg Jameson is often referred to as an internet pioneer. He has been called "America's leading expert on marketing like Amazon." The #1 best-selling author of multiple books, he is a sought-after consultant and speaker whose goal is to make you successful on the internet. He has awards for international developer of the year, Colorado Small Business of the Year and listed on the INC 500 of fastest growing companies in America.

Greg is the father of four grown children. He lives with his wife, Jill in the beautiful state of Colorado.

For speaking engagements or business consulting, contact Greg at 877-924-1414 or

greg@gregjameson.com.

Visit www.WebStoresLtd.com for further information.